INTRODUCTION

This book has been written as a basic introduction to the origins of the Church of Ireland and its present day role in society. It may be of use to young and old alike but has been written particularly with youth groups, confirmation groups and school classes in mind.

Three main areas are looked at:

1. The birth of Christianity

2. The history of the Church of Ireland

3. The beliefs and current practice of the Church of Ireland.

The book is designed so that it can either be read continuously or by reading each chapter separately. Bear in mind that the history is written very broadly and so many major historical events only get a brief mention. There are plenty of other books that will fill in the gaps!

Finally, while this book will present a history and identity from a Church of Ireland perspective, it is only one perspective – the author's. I have written in a way that I hope will provide an interesting perspective on this history but also with the aim of encouraging people to ask questions and dig deeper.

....

Andrew Brannigan (April 2010)

CONTENTS
SECTION 1 AND 2

SECTION 1

SECTION 2

CONTENTS
SECTION 3

SECTION 3

Old Testament [or] 'B.C.'

Christian belief is based on a collection of writings, letters and books that together are known as the Bible. The church holds that the Bible is 'God-breathed' – containing words that God has inspired people to write down. It is split into 2 parts:

39 & 27

BOOKS
of the Old Testament

BOOKS
of the New Testament

The Old Testament famously starts with the story of creation (In the beginning...) with the first man and woman and how they became separated from God by committing the first sin. What follows is an epic story of how God tries to restore this relationship with His people over many generations.

The Old Testament contains books on the laws given by God (e.g. The 10 Commandments), poetry, hymns and wisdom and the history of the Jewish people. It also contains books by the prophets – men who delivered messages from God to the people about their behaviour (mostly bad behaviour!) and also messages preparing for the coming of a Messiah or Christ.

In some places the Old Testament is a list of long forgotten laws and family trees. In other places it is a story of battle, blood, heroes and villains. Of love, lust, betrayal and redemption.

Some of the laws given to people in the Old Testament can seem pretty outlandish today (You could be put to death for being a rebellious young person!). However they can generally be divided up into 3 types to be better understood.

CEREMONIAL LAW: Which related specifically to how the Jews worshipped God (e.g. Leviticus 1). As this law was to help point towards the coming Christ and is fulfilled in him it is no longer applicable since His death and resurrection.

CIVIL LAW: These were designed for smooth functioning of Jewish society at a particular time (e.g. Deuteronomy 24) and no longer apply directly to modern Christianity. Both the Ceremonial and Civil law however, do still reflect the nature of God, and many of their principles are still important.

MORAL LAW: This law was the direct command for all people at all times (e.g. the 10 Commandments in Exodus 20). It reveals the nature and will of God and is for the good of all people everywhere.

A SCALE MODEL OF THE TEMPLE IN JERUSALEM

The first sin (wrongdoing) was to eat some fruit from a tree! (often assumed to be an apple but we don't know.) However, it was from a tree that God had specifically forbidden Adam and Eve to touch.

It symbolised mankind's willingness (and freedom) to separate from the perfect life with God. Sin has been part of human life ever since.

THE OLDEST PERSON IN THE BIBLE, METHUSELAH, DIED WHEN HE WAS 969 YEARS OLD.

KING SOLOMON HAD OVER

700

WIVES

THE GREATEST WARRIOR IN THE BIBLE IS GIDEON. WITH 300 MEN, 300 TRUMPETS(!?), AND GOD, HE DEFEATED 135,000 MIDIANITES.

THE SHORTEST VERSE IN THE BIBLE SIMPLY SAYS 'JESUS WEPT'

THE GIANT GOLIATH WAS SUPPOSED TO BE OVER 9 AND A HALF FEET TALL. HE WAS KILLED BY DAVID WHO SLUNG A STONE AT HIS HEAD THEN CHOPPED IT OFF WITH GOLIATH'S SWORD.

ELIJAH CURSED A GROUP OF YOUTHS FOR CALLING HIM 'BALDHEAD' AND IMMEDIATELY 2 BEARS EMERGE FROM A NEARBY WOOD AND MAUL 42 OF THEM TO DEATH (2 KINGS 2).

GOD ENABLES A DONKEY TO SPEAK IN ORDER TO ASK ITS OWNER TO STOP BEATING IT (NUMBERS 22)

ISAIAH 52 & 53 LISTS MORE THAN 20 PROPHECIES (PREDICTIONS) ABOUT JESUS, ALL OF WHICH ARE TRUE.

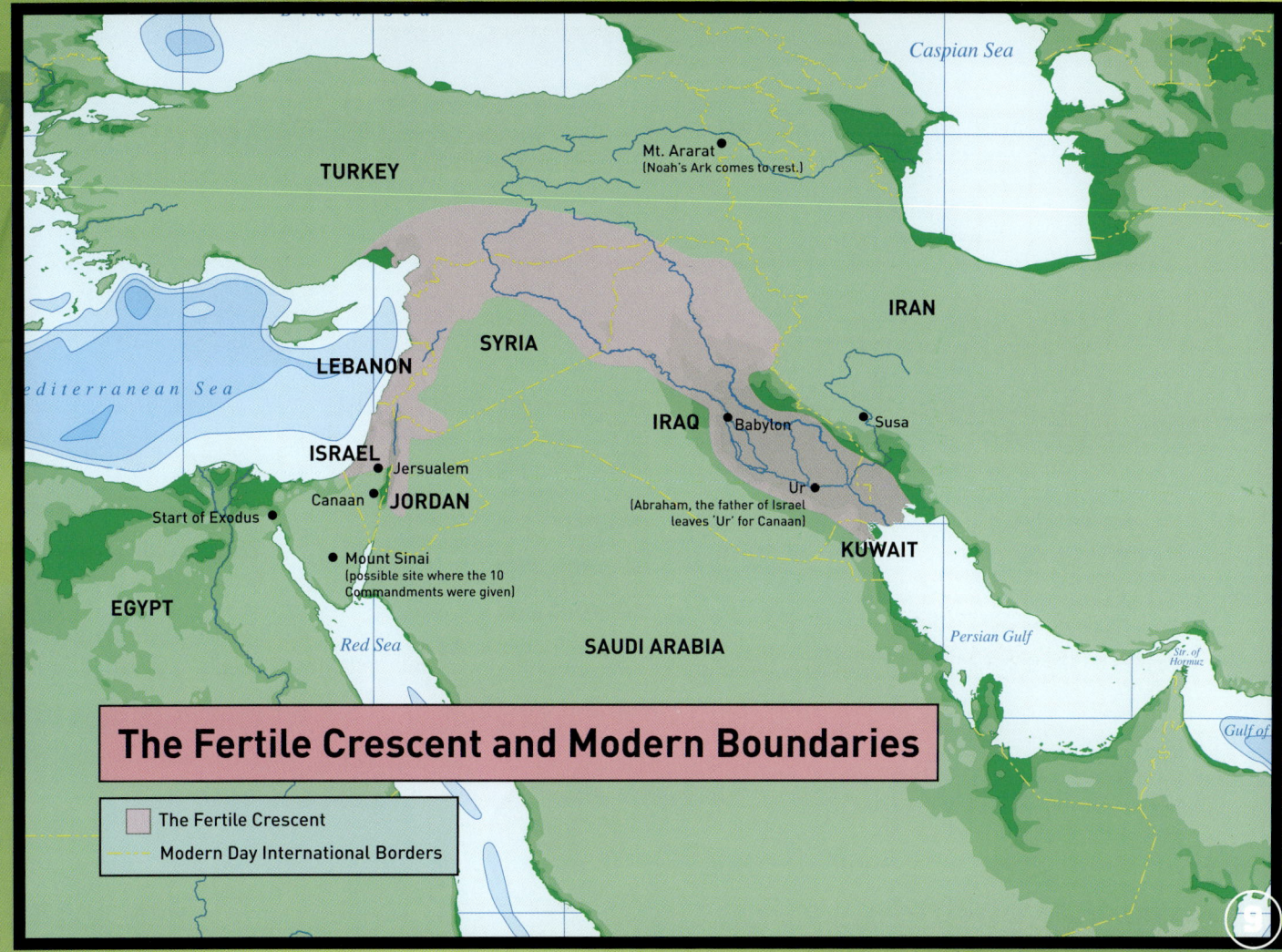

The Fertile Crescent and Modern Boundaries

Legend:
The Fertile Crescent
Modern Day International Borders

Map labels:
- Black Sea
- Caspian Sea
- TURKEY
- Mt. Ararat (Noah's Ark comes to rest.)
- IRAN
- SYRIA
- LEBANON
- Mediterranean Sea
- ISRAEL
- Jersualem
- Canaan
- JORDAN
- IRAQ
- Babylon
- Susa
- Ur (Abraham, the father of Israel leaves 'Ur' for Canaan)
- KUWAIT
- Start of Exodus
- Mount Sinai (possible site where the 10 Commandments were given)
- EGYPT
- Red Sea
- SAUDI ARABIA
- Persian Gulf
- Str. of Hormuz
- Gulf of

TIMELINE
OF THE OLD TESTAMENT

Moses leads the exodus from Egypt

David becomes King

Celts arrive in Ireland from Europe

Abraham enters Canaan

Judges begin to rule Israel

Jonah goes to Ninevah

Creation
(undated)

The Flood
(undated)

Saul becomes Israel's 1st King

1st people arrive in Ireland

Joseph sold into slavery

Kingdom splits into Israel and Judah

BIBLICAL EVENTS

7000BC	2500BC	2100BC	1900BC	1450BC	1375BC	1350BC	1050BC	1010BC	930BC	800BC	776BC

WORLD EVENTS

- Great Pyramid built in Egypt
- Stonehenge built
- Veterinary medicine invented
- Egyptian King Tutankhamen dies
- Coins first used in China
- Central heating first used in Korea
- The 'Illiad' and 'Odyssey' writte
- 1st Olympic Gam

Israel Conquered

2nd Temple built in Jerusalem

Jews revolt and found their own Kingdom

Herod the Great made puppet King of Judea

Jesus begins his ministry

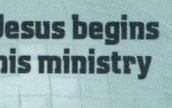

Jesus Crucified

Jews return from exile

Israel switches from Persian to Greek control

Jesus visits temple as a boy

Romans conquer Israel

Ireland organised into kingdoms

Judah falls and Jews exiled to Babylon

Rise of the Irish Kings

Jesus Born

Apostle Paul begins first missionary journey

722BC	586BC	538BC	509BC	312BC	165BC	63BC	55BC	37BC	6BC	6AD	27AD	30AD	45AD	70AD

- Romans build first paved road

- England conquered by Rome

- London founded

- Rome becomes a republic

- Augustus Caesar born

- Zealots revolt against Rome

- First solar eclipse predicted

The Birth & Early Years [of] Jesus

The Prophets of the Old Testament had foretold that the Jews would be sent a Messiah, who would deliver them from their oppressors or enemies.

Around 4BC this Messiah arrived. His name was Jesus Christ and He was born in a stable in Bethlehem, largely unnoticed by the world around him.

Crucially however, this was a miracle birth. For Jesus was conceived in Mary's womb by the Holy Spirit of God. He was God's Son, but also Mary's son, therefore both fully God and fully human. He was also born with a mission to complete, 'to save people from their sins' (be their saviour) and restore their relationship with God.

He was predicted to be a King (Zechariah 9:9) but it wasn't a very royal start! It was a humble birth into a poor family and under a death threat from the regional King Herod that caused the family to flee to Egypt.

Eventually though, they returned and Jesus was raised in the small town of Nazareth, where he became a carpenter.

We know very little about His early life except that when He was 12 years old he debated faith in the Temple in Jerusalem with an understanding that 'amazed'(Luke 2:47) the Teachers of Religion.

He is also recorded as being obedient to His parents and that he 'grew in wisdom and stature and in favour with God and people'. (Luke 2:52)

THERE ARE

HUNDREDS'

OF NAMES THAT HAVE BEEN USED TO DESCRIBE JESUS CHRIST; **LORD**, SAVIOUR, **MESSIAH**, LAMB OF GOD, **LIGHT OF THE WORLD**, MEDIATOR, LIVING WATER, KING, BREAD OF LIFE, BEGINNING AND END, **THE WAY, TRUTH AND LIFE**

: NAMES THAT HAVE A PERSONAL SIGNIFICANCE TO EACH CHRISTIAN

HOW COULD JESUS HAVE BEEN BORN IN 4 B.C. ('BEFORE CHRIST')?! SIMPLY PUT, THE CHRISTIAN CALENDAR WAS STARTED BY THE CHURCH IN THE 6TH CENTURY AND ALTHOUGH THEY WANTED IT TO START WITH THE BIRTH OF JESUS THEY GOT THEIR DATES WRONG!

'B.C.' MEANS 'BEFORE CHRIST' AND 'A.D.' MEANS 'ANNO DOMINI' –TRANSLATED AS 'IN THE YEAR OF OUR LORD'. THERE IS NO YEAR '0' IN THIS SYSTEM SO IT WENT FROM 1B.C. TO 1A.D.

THE STAR OF BETHLEHEM WAS REPORTED BY MATTHEW, BUT **AT THE SAME TIME CHINESE ASTRONOMERS RECORDED IT TOO.** TO THE CHINESE IT WAS A BRIGHT, UNKNOWN STAR

THE OT HAS OVER

300 PROPHECIES

ABOUT THE COMING OF JESUS CHRIST –FROM WHERE HE WOULD BE BORN (MICAH 5:2) RIGHT THROUGH TO HOW MUCH WOULD BE PAID TO BETRAY HIM
(30 PIECES OF SILVER IN ZECHARIAH 11:12-13)

13

The Ministry [of] Jesus

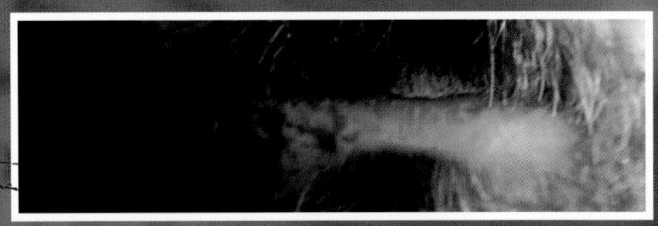

At 30 years of age Jesus preached a controversial sermon in his hometown synagogue (a meeting place for Jewish people). Quoting in the Scriptures from a prophecy (Isaiah 61) about the coming Messiah he simply said that he was the Messiah. The people there were absolutely furious that someone they had known since childhood would claim such a thing – they even tried to kill him but were unsuccessful.

From this point onwards His mission had started. He gathered disciples (those who followed him to learn from him) from all sorts of backgrounds and picked 12 to work more closely with him. They travelled around the country as Jesus preached a 'New Life' (John 10:10) for people – that by believing, asking to be forgiven and following him they would receive an eternal life now and beyond our earthly life.

Jesus illustrated this message with simple and memorable stories and demonstrated the power of his words with many miracles such as the feeding of 5,000 people from one small basket of food.

Yet despite this, he often shunned publicity, not wanting people to follow him for the wrong motives or try to use him to overthrow the Romans. Instead he was often to be found in the company of those rejected from society – lepers, prostitutes, tax collectors and people from different cultures.

Jesus healed people, forgave their sins, challenged them to follow him and live a better life. He still does. He was the fulfilment of the Old Testament laws and God's message of salvation to every person. However he would not get long to show it.

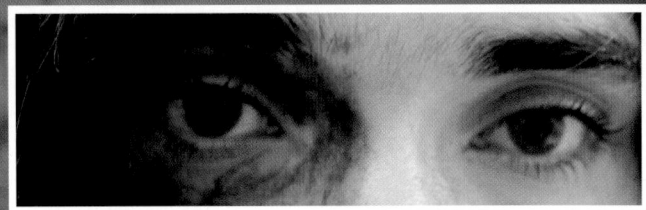

LUNATIC, LIAR OR LORD?

As Jesus claimed to be God on earth there are only really 3 options as to how we treat him:
1. LUNATIC: Jesus was not God, but he mistakenly believed that he was.
2. LIAR: Jesus was not God, and he knew it, but he said so anyway.
3. LORD: Jesus is God.

So was Jesus mad in thinking he was God's Son, bad in deceiving us or actually God's son. What do you think?

GOD OR MAN?

Jesus was both God and human and so displayed many of the emotions that you and I do. He knew deep pain and sorrow, he knew how to rejoice and often got frustrated and even angry to the point of violence but, crucially as God, never committed sin.

ATTITUDE TOWARDS WOMEN

Jesus was born into a culture that viewed women and children as property and forcibly shunned the sick and disabled. Jesus' accepting attitude and interaction with these people (and many other outcasts) was not only revolutionary then, but it still is today.

TEENAGE REBELLION?

It is probable that at least some of the disciples were only teenagers. Perhaps as young as 14! Read some of the stories associated with the disciples and imagine being there as a young person!

AND I WOULD WALK 200 MILES...

Jesus' entire ministry took place between the age of 30 and 33. During it He never travelled more than 200 miles from where He was born.

The Death & Resurrection [of] Jesus

By the third year of Jesus' mission the Jewish religious leaders were plotting to arrest him. They were fed up with his claims, his popularity and his criticism of them (He called them hypocrites). Eventually He was arrested by the religious leaders in Jerusalem, taken to Pontius Pilate (the Roman in charge of the region) and accused of undermining Roman rule. Pilate found him innocent but under pressure from a Jewish mob handed him over to be crucified. He would then have to suffer an agonizing and humiliating death on a cross beside two thieves. (To this day Christians around the world hold to the cross as a symbol of their faith in Christ.)

Three days after his death however, an event took place upon which the whole of Christianity is based. Jesus Christ rose from the dead and appeared to many people. This was called the Resurrection and is something that Christians regard, not just as a belief, but also as a fact of history.

The Bible tells us that after he was raised from the dead Jesus stayed on earth and appeared to His followers and others for 40 days before leaving them and ascending to heaven. They would not be left alone however but would be given a 'helper' – the Holy Spirit of God.

THE GARDEN TOMB

THE HISTORICAL EVIDENCE FOR JESUS.

The life and death of Jesus is recorded by other sources beyond the Bible. The historian Josephus refers to him as a 'wise man that drew to himself many Jews' and also as someone who performed many miracles. Other sources refer to the movement of Christians that sprang up soon afterwards. There is also historical evidence of the darkness over the land that accompanied His death.

THE COURT CASE FOR RESURRECTION.

We know that Jesus lived, died and was buried. We know that the Romans and other leaders wanted this new religion dead. Yet we also know that the body went missing, then appeared newly alive to hundreds of people. Within days the church was born despite heavy persecution. The conclusion we must seriously consider is that Jesus rose from the grave. The implications of this for you and me are monumental. *If it is true that Jesus rose from the dead and is alive today, what does that mean for us?*

Crucifixion was an ancient method of execution that was designed to be as painful and drawn out as possible (it could take days to die). It was also used as a public humiliation for the victims and their families.

Where exactly did Jesus die? The Gospel writers call the place where Jesus was crucified Golgotha—an Aramaic word meaning "the skull." Calvary is the Latin form of the word. No-one knows today exactly where this site was except that it was on a hill.

Birth of the Church

The disciples had been ready to give up their new faith upon the arrest and crucifixion of Jesus. They had already abandoned him, they were scattered and in fear of their lives. Suddenly though, with His resurrection and appearance before them, they were transformed and immediately began to preach the Gospel ('Good news') to others. Just 10 days after the ascension of Christ to Heaven around 120 of these followers were gathered together in Jerusalem when the promised gift of the Holy Spirit arrived. The Holy Spirit came upon them like a mighty wind and each disciple looked as if tongues of fire had settled upon them and they were also able to speak in different languages. Many other Jews, seeing what was happening and then having Christ explained to them, also became believers. That day (Pentecost) 3,000 were baptised and the Church was born.

However this fledging church was immediately under threat from the Pharisees (a highly religious and powerful section of the Jewish society) and before long Christians were being arrested and even executed. Chief among the persecutors was a man named Saul. Saul had been there when the first martyr, Stephen, was stoned to death but on his way to Damascus to persecute more Christians, Jesus spoke to him and he converted to the Christian Faith becoming Paul. The subsequent teaching and missionary journeys of Paul helped to expand the church across Europe and also to Gentiles (non-Jews).

ST. STEPHEN- HE WAS THE FIRST DISCIPLE TO BE PERSECUTED FOR HIS FAITH

HOW DOES THE HOLY SPIRIT WORK?

The Holy Spirit is God giving us 'power from on high' (Luke 24:49) and was key to the formation of the church. The Holy Spirit works in Christians and with Christians. He helps them live out their faith, resist temptation and also produces good 'fruit' in their lives.

CHURCH?

The first churches where characterised, not by buildings, but by what Christians did. They sold their possessions to give to the poor. They preached the good news and many were added to their number. They met up in the temple courts every day and also in each other's homes – where they would 'break bread' (Similar to a Communion service) in remembrance of Jesus. (See Acts 2:42-47)

WHAT IS THE HOLY TRINITY?

God is referred to in the Bible as Father, Son and Holy Spirit - 3 separate descriptions of the one God with the one purpose. The Trinity consists of God, our Father in heaven; Jesus His Son, revealed on earth (and now glorified in heaven); and God the Holy Spirit, moving among us here and now. Not 3 gods but 3 persons in one God.

Pentecost literally means **'THE FIFTIETH DAY'** as it took place 50 days after the **RESURRECTION OF CHRIST**

19

New Testament

The first Christians passed on the Faith by word of mouth, recounting what was seen and heard of Jesus' ministry. However, as those who had lived alongside Jesus began to die it became important to get a written account of His life.

The first 4 books of the New Testament describe the life of Christ – written from different angles 'according to' Matthew and John (of the 12 disciples) and also Mark and Luke (who were other followers of Christ). These 4 books became known as the Gospels and were probably written around 30-60 years after Christ's death.

In addition, Luke also wrote an account of the early church called the Acts of the Apostles (an Apostle was a disciple that Jesus sent to do teaching and missionary work). Various letters were also written to churches (such as 'Romans', to the church in Rome) to encourage them and challenge them to faithful living and to focus on Jesus Christ. The apostle Paul wrote most of these including some letters to individuals such as 'Timothy'.

Most of these books (the letters were also known as books) were widely accepted as scripture from the moment they were first read but it would be almost 300 years before the church agreed to the exact list of 27 books that make up the New Testament today.

CAVES OF QUMRAN - COPIES OF THE SCRIPTURES WERE DISCOVERED HERE IN 1947

ARE THERE ANY 'DA VINCI CODE'-TYPE WRITINGS?

As the Christian church spread, lots of different viewpoints and splinter groups arose that moved quite far from mainstream Christian thinking. One movement in particular were called the Gnostics and they produced various writings including the 'Gospel of Thomas'. However they were so far removed from the accepted Gospels of Matthew, Mark, Luke and John that they were regarded as simply fictitious. The early church quickly rejected them from what became regarded as correct or 'orthodox' Christian belief.

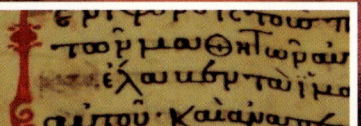

LANGUAGES OF THE BIBLE.

The OT was written in the Hebrew language while the NT was written in Greek. Jesus, however, would have spoken mostly the local language of Aramaic.

HOW DO NT TEXTS COMPARE IN ACCURACY TO OTHER TEXTS?

Very well! For instance the Roman Emperor Caesar's 'Gallic war' manuscript has copies dating back to around 850AD (900 years after they would have been written) and there are only around 10 surviving. In contrast most of the New Testament was written within 100 years of the crucifixion of Christ and there are over 5,500 surviving manuscripts – some dating to less than 100 years after the events they describe.

Christianity becomes Official

For the first 300 years of the Church, Christians were heavily persecuted for their beliefs. Thousands of them were killed through stoning, crucifixion, being burnt alive and even being fed to lions and other wild animals. Often they would be killed in a stadium watched by the public. However despite this, very few Christians denied their faith and the example of those that were martyred (killed because they wouldn't give up their beliefs) led to even more following Christ. The church became stronger and stronger.

By the time of the Roman emperor Constantine almost 300 years after Christ's death, the Christian Church was firmly established across the Roman Empire. While previously many emperors had actively persecuted Christians, Constantine was the first emperor to give Christianity official recognition as a religion.

Also at this time the Canon (or list) of New Testament books was agreed and a statement of faith was drawn up by church leaders at a meeting in Nicaea (in modern Turkey). This statement helped Christians everywhere to better understand and agree on their faith and today it is known as the Nicene Creed.

Christianity was now, in a sense, official and Christians would continue from this point to shape the entire world.

STATUE OF CONSTANTINE: The torso made of bronze and wood has been lost.

WERE CHRISTIANS ACTUALLY 'THROWN TO THE LIONS'?

In the capital city of Rome all sorts of gory spectacles were regularly put on (in places like the Colosseum – which still stands in modern Rome). Gladiator combat, animal combat and executions were popular with Roman citizens. Christians and other prisoners would have been placed in amphitheatres (open-air arenas) with various animals such as savage dogs, bears, wild boars and yes - even lions and other wildcats.

ROMAN AMPHITHEATRE AT HERAPOLIS

FOUNDING FATHER

A founding father of the church: Polycarp, the Bishop of Smyrna (Izmir in Turkey) was taught by the Apostle John (a disciple of Jesus) and became an important leader of the church – especially in combating the many heresies (false beliefs) surrounding Christian faith at that time. Like many Christians he was tried in public for his faith. Asked to revile Christ he replied, "Eighty-six years have I served him, and He never did me any wrong. How then can I blaspheme my King who saved me?' He was put to death by burning at the stake. Despite this, more and more people became Christians.

SEPARATION OF JEWS AND CHRISTIANS

While the vast majority of early converts to Christianity were Jewish it became much more a faith of the Gentiles (non-Jews). Over this period Jews and Christians went their separate ways and so even today the Jewish people still wait on their prophesised Messiah.

TRIED AS ATHEISTS

Many Christian martyrs were actually tried as atheists for refusing to acknowledge the pagan gods of the Roman Empire. Such was the strength of their belief in Jesus though, few denied him, even on pain of death.

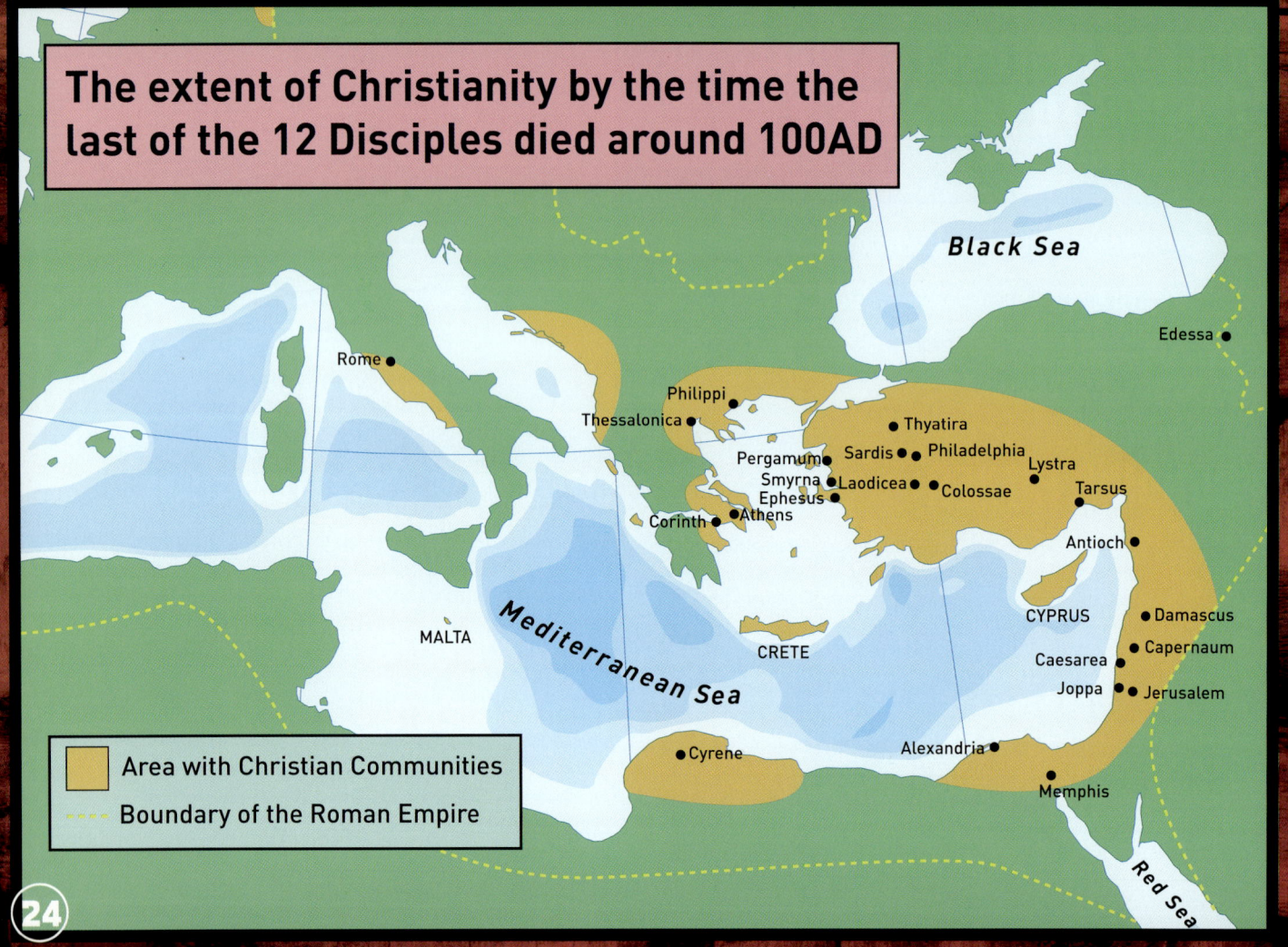

The extent of Christianity by the time the last of the 12 Disciples died around 100AD

Black Sea

Edessa

Rome

Philippi

Thessalonica

Thyatira

Pergamum   Sardis   Philadelphia

Smyrna   Laodicea   Lystra

Ephesus   Colossae   Tarsus

Corinth   Athens

Antioch

CYPRUS   Damascus

MALTA   Capernaum

Mediterranean Sea   Caesarea

CRETE   Joppa   Jerusalem

Cyrene   Alexandria

Memphis

Red Sea

Area with Christian Communities

Boundary of the Roman Empire

24

The Spread of Christianity by the time of the Council of Nicaea 325AD and the time of the death of Saint Patrick around 460AD

North Sea

• Downpatrick

BRITAIN

Atlantic Ocean

GAUL
• Poitiers

Black Sea

SPAIN

ITALY
Rome •

Constantinople •
• Nicaea

ANATOLIA

SYRIA

GREECE
Corinth •

Antioch •

Mediterranean Sea

Hippo •

JUDEA

Jerusalem

Alexandria •

EGYPT

Red

Christian Areas, 325AD
Additional Christian Areas, 460AD
- - - - Boundary of the Roman Empire, 395AD

25

Christianity comes to Ireland

The Roman Empire, while successfully invading England and Wales, had never actually managed to conquer (and therefore bring Christianity to) Ireland. In fact it was the Irish who often invaded Britain! - if only to raid the coastal areas for plunder and slaves. It was on one of these raids that a young 16-year-old Christian called Patrick was captured. Patrick was sold as a slave and had to work as a shepherd around the area of Slemish in County Antrim. He recounted that he had to endure great hardship but would find comfort in prayer.

Eventually Patrick escaped to France where he trained as a priest and soon realised that he was being called to preach Christ to the pagan (non-Christian) Irish. He eventually got permission to travel back on a missionary journey and founded the first Church in Ireland outside Downpatrick at Saul in 432A.D. Over perhaps the next 30 years he dedicated his life to travelling around what was a wild and often dangerous Ireland, preaching and praying. The Kings of Ireland were converted from the previous ancient beliefs like Druidism and Christianity was established as the official religion. By becoming Christian, Ireland moved from being a distant, unruly outpost to be more closer tied to the rest of Europe through a common church.

It was also at this time that what we know as the first parishes were formed, served by priests - who were themselves under the care and guidance of Bishops.

STATUE OF SAINT PATRICK

PARISH

A parish is a local area served by a church under the responsibility of a Priest. Some parishes can have more than one church building and even several clergy and other staff.

PRIEST

Priests are people who have been ordained (set apart) to undertake various religious functions and duties. These include the pastoral care of the people contained within a parish and the undertaking of church services. In the Church of Ireland some ceremonies such as Holy Communion can only be led by a priest.

BISHOP

The role of a bishop dates back to the early church and comes from the Greek word meaning 'overseer'. It is regarded as a position of authority (a bishop ordains priests) and oversight in the church. A bishop will generally administer a diocese -which is an area of parishes. One of the roles attributed to bishops is that of shepherd of the flock – imagery that can be still be seen today as each bishop will carry a shepherds crook at a church service.

WHY THE SHAMROCK?

Patrick had to explain the Holy Trinity – the idea of a three-part but single God – to the Irish. Legend has it that he picked up a Shamrock and used its leaves to explain the mystery of the Holy Trinity. That linked together perfectly in one plant were 3 leaves – one each for God the Father, Son and Holy Spirit.

THE IRISH DIDN'T JUST NAME IRELAND.

The origins of the name Scotland come from the Latin word 'Scoti' – used to name the Irish raiders that came often to the shores of Britain. Eventually one of these tribes settled in NW Scotland and it became known as the land of the Scots –Scotland therefore was named after the Irish!

Saints & Scholars

Alongside many of these new churches sprang up **monasteries.** A monastery was a place where men devoted themselves, as monks, to a life of prayer and worship but also to serve the poor and sick. Monasteries were the first places in Ireland that provided for education (such as reading and writing) and would often be the only places willing to receive weary travellers or the sick.

Fairly soon the work of Irish Monasteries was recognised as the best in the world – they were famous for their devotion, desire to spread the message of Christ and dedication to studying the Bible. They built libraries and produced beautifully illustrated manuscripts of the Bible including the Book of Kells – regarded by many as the finest treasure in Ireland.

Many of these Irish Christian leaders (we now call them 'saints' in recognition of their achievements) undertook missionary journeys to continue spreading Christianity throughout the British Isles and Europe. One of them, Saint Brendan, was even rumoured to have reached America! We do know however, that across Europe today there are still monasteries that were founded by such saints as Columbanas, Colum Cille, Brendan and Gall. Europe for about 500 years after the fall of the Roman Empire (from around 450AD onwards) was in the midst of the **'Dark Ages'** when much previous learning and Christian knowledge was almost lost. The work of Irish monks and missionaries helped to preserve this learning and religion across Europe.

MONASTERY AT CLONMACNOISE

Such was the growth of Christianity in Ireland, and the work of the monasteries in particular, that it became known as the land of Saints and Scholars.

BOOK OF KELLS

Produced in the 9th Century, the Book of Kells contains the 4 Gospels of the Bible in Latin and is the best example of an illuminated (illustrated) manuscript anywhere in the world. It is on display at Trinity College, Dublin.

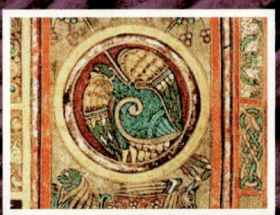

THE PEN IS DEADLIER THAN THE SWORD

The Irish Monk John Scotus Eriugena was reputed to have been killed in 870AD when he was hacked to death with sharpened pens by students he had forced to think too much!

WHAT IS A MONASTERY?

A church was a building that served a local community with a priest in charge. A Bishop would have looked after many priests. A monastery had a slightly different focus to a church and they tended to be fewer, but also bigger and wealthier. This meant that sometimes the Abbot in charge of a monastery would become the leader of the local Christians rather than the Bishop.

THE LIFE OF A MONK

The monks may have lived a simple and prayerful life but they also were highly intellectual. They developed centres of learning in reading, writing (particularly in Latin), history, agricultural skills, medicine, music, poetry, art and of course in understanding the Bible. Learning with monks was a high privilege and Irish Monasteries would been regarded as the world's best universities of their day.

Ireland Invaded

While the Romans never invaded Ireland, the **Vikings** did. They came (around 795AD) in Long Ships from Scandinavia initially just to look for riches and then go home. The Irish church had become famous and stories of its treasure and riches had spread across Europe. Therefore its churches and monasteries became prime targets and many were plundered and destroyed with their priests and monks killed. The church could do little to defend itself and soon declined as a centre for European Christianity.

By around 850AD Vikings started to build settlements and live in Ireland permanently – they started what would become the cities of Dublin, Cork, limerick, Waterford and Wexford. For over 200 years the Vikings and the Kings of Ireland fought each other with no clear winner until gradually the Vikings began to convert to Christianity and take on Irish customs. The Irish didn't so much get rid of Vikings as make them Irish!

Once again, however, in 1170 Ireland was invaded. This time by the Norman Earl, **Strongbow**. The Normans had only recently conquered England and Wales and acquiring Ireland was seen as a way to gain more power and riches.

Strongbow took Dublin and the area around it and slowly, over the next few hundred years, the whole of Ireland would be conquered and come under the control of the English King. The rule of law and way of life in Ireland would undergo radical changes and it would be more or less under the direct control of England or Great Britain until 1922.

WHO WERE THE IRISH?

Who are the Irish? This is a good question!
Originally they were a Celtic people –sharing
ancestry with others from Europe and moving into
Scotland . Gradually there was an inter-mingling
with the Vikings, then with the Normans (from
Northern France) and Anglo-Saxon English and
Welsh (themselves descended from places like
Germany and Denmark). To be Irish today means
that you probably have descendants from about a
dozen different countries!

DO IT THE MEDIEVAL WAY

Strongbow was persuaded to come to Ireland by the
disposed Irish King Mac Mourrough. He did it the
usual medieval way – by giving Strongbow lots of
cash and his daughter's hand in marriage!

WHO WERE THE VIKINGS?

Who were the Vikings? Well they weren't actually called
Vikings! – the name we use refers to what they did. To go 'a
viking' meant to go on a raid. They were from modern day
Scandinavia –particularly Norway and Denmark and were
excellent sailors (they discovered Iceland) and fighters.

They were also famous for their legends (like Beowulf),
poems and various gods like Odin. They believed that if you
died peacefully you went to 'Hel' (which for them was not
hot but cold) and if you died gloriously in battle you went to
Valhalla (heaven). Most Vikings though had converted to
Christianity by the end of 11th Century.

IRISH ROUND TOWERS

Dotted around Ireland near
medieval churches & monastic
sites there are the ruins of
around 100 Round Towers and
almost 20 complete towers
(not bad considering most are
over 1000 years old!). They
are fairly unique in Europe and
were probably built as bell
towers, rather than refuges
from the Vikings.

ROUND TOWER AT ARDMORE

Popes, Bishops, Dioceses & Parishes

KING HENRY II

The 12th Century in Ireland also witnessed a great change in how the Church operated. The Irish church, while outwardly loyal to the Vatican in Rome, had always been fairly independent and so didn't always obey the rules that came from the Vatican. For instance Irish clergy continued to get married when the Vatican specifically forbade it.

The head of the Church in Western Europe, the Pope, wanted to tie the Irish Church closer to the authority of the Vatican and he used his immense influence to persuade the English **King Henry II** to ensure that this happened. In 1171 the church was reorganised to bring it in line with the rest of Europe. This was followed a few years later by the establishment of 24 areas or dioceses that would be administered by a Bishop. Many of these Dioceses are still in existence today.

An immense change however was that the Church had now become an established or state church tied closely to the Pope and the Normans. It was run the same way as the English church and so became anglicised or Anglican. It was also more stable and organised and had a large degree of influence, even over the Irish Kings. By the end of the 12th Century it had become probably the most important national institution in the life of the Irish people.

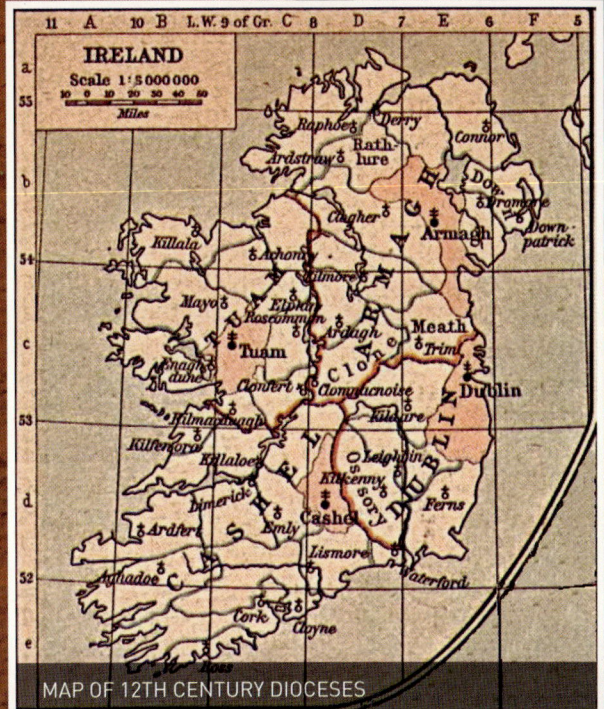

MAP OF 12TH CENTURY DIOCESES

BEYOND THE PALE

England ruled Ireland 'officially' but the reality for quite some time was that the Irish were still doing their own thing, and this meant constant attacks on the English! In the 1400's the English and Anglo-Irish were mostly to be found in the fortified area around Dublin called the Pale. To be in it was to viewed as under the rule of law and those outside it were seen as wild and uncivilised. This is where we get the expression 'Beyond the Pale' as something unacceptable.

Passport To Being A Bishop

The English didn't just reorganise the Irish church; they effectively took it over. Over time all the Bishops appointed would have to be English and it even became illegal for an Irishman to hold a position of power in a church. This was certainly one way of making it more Anglican!

THE ENGLISH BECOME IRISH

One of the problems for the English Crown was that those English who settled in Ireland often adopted Irish customs and became indistinguishable from the Irish. To put a stop to this new laws were introduced to make them (and the native Irish) more English. They were not allowed to: speak, dress or write in Irish, use an Irish form of a name or play Irish games. For the Anglo-Irish it was illegal to marry anyone Irish or even have an Irish poet or musician in their house! Not surprisingly these laws were widely ignored.

The Reformation in Ireland

MARTIN LUTHER

By the 1500's, Christianity in Europe was in turmoil. Many Christians were tired of corruption within the church and others were beginning to emphasise a personal relationship with God, rather than having to go through the church as an institution. This was still a time when the ordinary person had no access to a Bible and sermons were preached in Latin and so nobody could understand them!

Reform of the church was demanded and a major movement led by the German, Martin Luther, became known as the Reformation. This led to a major split from the Roman Catholic church (called so because the Pope was based in Rome) and its followers who 'protested' against the Vatican became known as Protestants.

At the same time **King Henry VIII** of England (and also much of Ireland) was having marriage problems... His first wife had not given him a male heir and he wanted to divorce her. The Church wouldn't permit this and so the answer was simple – break away from the authority of the Pope and run things yourself. Henry declared himself the head of the Church in 1534 and the Church of England started the gradual transition to becoming a Protestant church.

In Ireland the Reformation hadn't really taken hold but Henry, having declared himself also head of the Irish Church, decided to impose it upon the Irish. Initially there was little change but when Henry set about dissolving the Monasteries by taking their land and property the Reformation in Ireland was seen to be another way of exerting English control. So while many Irish accepted it superficially, they still remained in allegiance to the Pope. However, the established Church of Ireland, being closely tied to England, was now a Protestant Church.

CATCH ME IF YOU CAN

The Reformation didn't catch on everywhere though. It spread mostly through northern Europe and so even today it is countries like England, Scotland, Germany, Denmark and Finland that are largely Protestant and southern European countries like Spain, Italy and Portugal that are Roman Catholic.

PRESBYTERIANS

During the Reformation the official Church of Scotland adopted a Presbyterian form of Protestantism. As many of the settlers (particularly to Ulster) came from Scotland, they brought Presbyterian churches with them. Pretty soon Presbyterianism was the largest Protestant 'denomination' in Ulster, and still is today.

INDULGE YOURSELF

Martin Luther (and many others) were enraged at the corrupt church practice of selling 'Indulgences' – a supposed method of granting freedom from God's punishment in exchange for money. On 1517 he nailed his response to these church abuses (called 'The 95 Theses') onto the door of the Castle Church in Germany, so starting the Reformation.

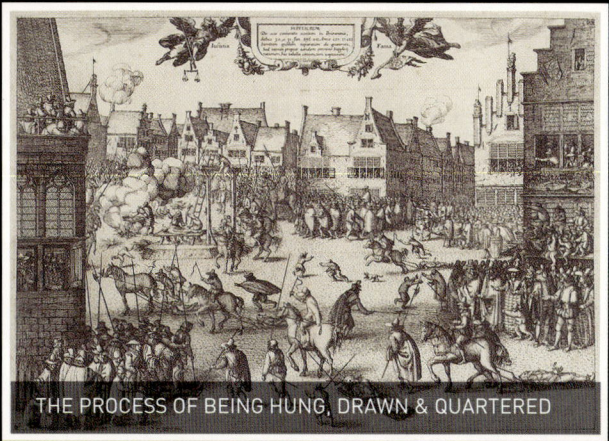

THE PROCESS OF BEING HUNG, DRAWN & QUARTERED

HUNG, DRAWN AND QUARTERED

Henry VIII was not the sort of King you would cross. Of his 6 wives he had 2 executed and the leaders of the Irish rebellion were hung, drawn and quartered - a most grisly death involving being drawn through the streets to a gallows, being hung there until half dead and then cut into pieces while still alive. It helped to persuade others not to rebel!

Rebellion, Persecution & more Invasions

Despite their best efforts the English made little progress in Ireland with the Reformation. There was a new official **prayer book** but it was in English and rejected by most of the population. The Pope still appointed Roman Catholic Bishops for Ireland but they had no power over an English controlled church and generally lived abroad.

Therefore the English had a new idea to bring Protestantism to Ireland –they would 'plant' people from Britain into Ireland with the promise of land that would be taken mainly from Irish Roman Catholics. This became known as **the Plantations**. Many of these settlers came to Ulster from Scotland and were part of a new branch of the Church called Presbyterianism. The plantations radically changed what is now Northern Ireland into a majority Protestant region.

In 1641 a major Irish rebellion took place which led to the death of many Protestants (mostly new settlers) and this led the new (non-royal) leader of Britain, **Oliver Cromwell**, to invade. Cromwell hated Roman Catholicism and also had no love for Anglicanism. By 1650, through war, famine and disease it is thought he almost halved the population. He then settled Ireland with more English and by 1660 Catholics only owned around 20% of the land.

The Church of Ireland also suffered under Cromwell and again with the Catholic King James II in 1685. This changed with the success of **King William of Orange** in 1690 and then the Catholic (and also Presbyterian) population had to endure harsh **Penal Laws** that deprived them of wealth, education and power but at least leaving them their religious freedom. At the expense of others, the Church of Ireland rose to an ascendency in Irish affairs.

OLIVER CROMWELL

27 OUT OF 30 AIN'T BAD

The early 1600's were not a great time for the Church of Ireland. There weren't enough clergy and a lack of education and supervision for them. Churches fell into ruin. One notorious Archbishop, McGrath, had the right to appoint clergy to 30 parishes. He gave 27 of them to his sons!

BONJOUR!

The French arrive. In the late 1600's the French Protestant Huguenots, under severe persecution in Catholic France, fled to other countries. Around 10,000 (quite a number back then) settled in Ireland and many Irish Protestants today will probably have some French heritage.

THE CHURCH DULLS DOWN

Cromwell forced upon the Church of Ireland a puritan form of Church government where Prayer Books and Bishops were forbidden and all churches had to have any decoration and ornaments removed and destroyed. It would make church a slightly duller place to be!

BATTLE OF THE BOYNE 1690

KING BILLY & THE ORANGE

When King James II came to the throne in 1685 he wanted to make England and Ireland Catholic again. The majority Protestants in England therefore invited his (Protestant) sister Mary and her husband William to invade. They did so successfully and he became King in 1689. James II fled to Ireland to fight on there and was defeated at the river Boyne (near Drogheda) in 1690 by an army that included Irish Protestants. As King William's title had been 'Prince of Orange' this became the colour of the Irish loyalists.

37

Denominations & Disestablishment

The 18th & 19th Century

In 1801 the **Act of Union** united all of Britain and Ireland under one government. It also united the Church of Ireland and the Church of England. For the previous hundred years though quite a few people had grown impatient with the established churches and their perceived lack of care for the poor –particularly in the new cities that were springing up in the Industrial Revolution. One Anglican priest, John Wesley, travelled around Britain and Ireland preaching revival and when the Bishops' refused to ordain more preachers he decided to do it himself. The denomination of **Methodism** was born and Methodist churches slowly sprang up across Ireland.

The Roman Catholic Church continued to be the denomination of choice for the majority of Irish but during this time the Presbyterian Church continued to grow, particularly in the Ulster region.

The Church of Ireland also grew in this period but continued to be regarded unfavourably by many Irish as an arm of the English state –particularly as everyone had to pay **tithes** (tax on farming income) to the church.

FAMINE MEMORIAL, CUSTOM HOUSE QUAY, DUBLIN

In addition the **Potato Famine** of the 1840's (in which nearly 1 million people died) highlighted great injustices in land ownership. In recognition of these imbalances the Church of Ireland was slowly reorganised and in 1871 was **disestablished**, or separated, from the state. This meant that it would no longer enjoy a privileged position alongside state authorities. The Church of Ireland had to almost start again from scratch and so developed its own set of rules (or canons) and devised its own prayer book, both based upon but now separate from, the Church of England.

38

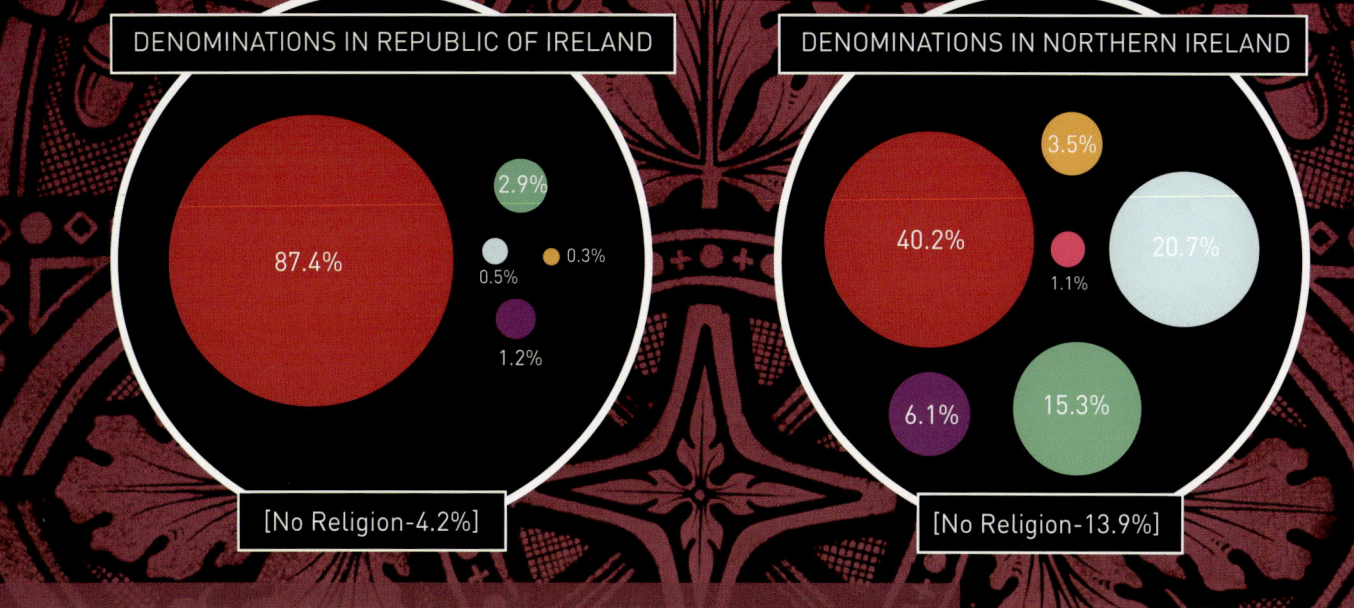

DENOMINATIONS IN REPUBLIC OF IRELAND

87.4%

2.9%

0.5% 0.3%

1.2%

[No Religion-4.2%]

DENOMINATIONS IN NORTHERN IRELAND

40.2%

3.5%

20.7%

1.1%

6.1% 15.3%

[No Religion-13.9%]

- 🔴 ROMAN CATHOLIC
- 🟢 CHURCH OF IRELAND
- ⚪ PRESBYTERIAN
- 🟡 METHODIST
- 🔴 BAPTIST
- 🟣 OTHER DENOMINATIONS

WHAT IS A DENOMINATION & WHY SO MANY?

"A denomination can be described as an organisation of Christian churches that subscribe to the same set of beliefs."

With the Reformation in the 16th Century several branches of Protestantism emerged from the Roman Catholic church and over the years more and more denominations have emerged from the Protestant church. Each has usually formed because they have a slightly different view on doctrine (belief) such as the importance of Baptism, or else a desire to be run and to worship in a different way. They will all tend to have much more in common however, with crucially the centrally held belief in Christ as Lord and Saviour.

The Republic [of] Ireland

By the turn of the 20th Century the desire for many Irish, particularly Roman Catholics, to be free from British rule had not lessened. While the British were trying to bring about a system of self-governance or 'Home Rule' in Ireland there was a lot of political upheaval taking place involving various different nationalist (wanting to break away from Britain) and unionist (wanting to remain joined) groups. **Irish Civil war** loomed but the outbreak of the First World War in 1914 prevented it from happening as so many Irish, both Protestant and Catholic, joined up to fight.

However, while the World War was halfway through, some nationalist groups were plotting a rebellion. On **Easter Monday 1916**, Nationalists took over key buildings in Dublin and declared a Republic. The rebellion was quickly crushed but it led to a lot of popular support and a longer guerrilla war (a smaller army using surprise and mobility against a larger force) took place until in 1921 a Treaty was signed whereby 26 majority Roman Catholic counties became an independent Irish Free State (eventually renamed the Republic of Ireland in 1948) and the 6 majority Protestant counties became Northern Ireland.

For the Church of Ireland this meant that many of its members moved from the south to a more Protestant Northern Ireland. However, even though there was some pressure to split north and south, it resisted and remains an all-Ireland church today.

GENERAL POST OFFICE, DUBLIN. The centre of the Easter Rising

ROYAL IRISH RIFLES IN TRENCHES AT THE BATTLE OF THE SOMME

TRAGEDY OF THE GREAT WAR

Despite the fact that there was no conscription in Ireland, over 200,000 men, both Catholic and Protestant, volunteered to fight alongside the English and French. Eventually 3 divisions of Irish were formed (around 45,000 men), 2 from the south and 1 from Ulster. Losses in this war were horrific (The Ulster division lost over a third of its men in just 2 days of the Somme battle) and across the Church of Ireland today you will often see plaques to commemorate the loss of (mostly young) men in this war.

SINN FEIN AND THE UVF

Contrary to how they are perceived today these two organisations formed as Ireland was to be given 'Home Rule' in 1914. The Ulster Volunteer Force (UVF) was formed to protect the way of life of Unionists in a Catholic dominated Ireland that was about to get its own parliament. It had a membership of over 100,000. Sinn Fein (meaning 'ourselves alone') were originally a fringe movement with few involved (For instance the Irish Volunteers, formed in response to the UVF, numbered over 180,000). They rose to prominence at the polls after the 1916 Easter Rising.

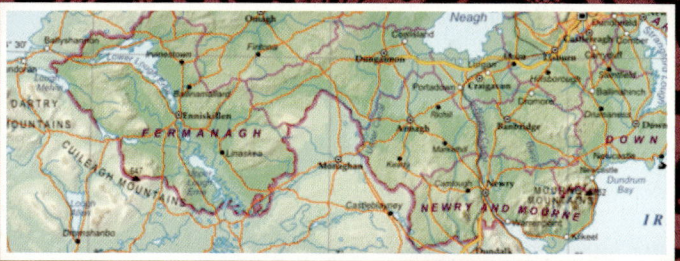

POPULATION MOVE

As the realisation hit many Church of Ireland Protestants that the island would be split into two countries, many of them moved to the 'six counties' –particularly those living closer to where the new border would be. In just a few years the Protestant population in the Republic of Ireland had dropped by over 30%.

Civil Strife!
Troubles in Northern Ireland

WALL MURAL FROM THE TROUBLES

Despite partition and the separately functioning governments north and south, a great deal of tension and suspicion continued between Protestants and Catholics, particularly in Northern Ireland. In the 1960s, with Catholics in Northern Ireland having little access to power, a **civil rights movement** started and protests were held. Violence between the two groups flared up and in 1969 British troops were sent to Northern Ireland to try and control the situation. However the violence escalated and over the next 30 years around 3,500 people would die in the killings and bombings that took place, particularly as a result of paramilitary groups. Political change came slowly but eventually progress was made and the **Good Friday Agreement** of 1998 led to a power sharing government of both Unionists and Nationalists and a huge reduction in sectarian (between religions) violence.

Throughout this time the Church of Ireland in Northern Ireland had to balance a mission to promote peace while at the same time serving its Protestant and largely Unionist membership. The fact that it had remained an all-Ireland church gave it a particular role and it was central to several reconciliation organisations that were formed. It has become a church with **reconciliation** as a major mission and much of this work is still ongoing today.

This was also a time of great population change and growth in Northern Ireland with many large housing estates being built. In response to this many established parishes, at great cost, built 'daughter churches' to serve this new housing. Over the years these churches became parishes in their own right and can often be recognised by their different shape and layout to the older and more traditional church buildings

THE SITE OF THE ENNISKILLEN BOMB IN 1987

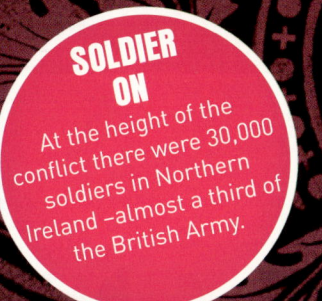

SOLDIER ON

At the height of the conflict there were 30,000 soldiers in Northern Ireland –almost a third of the British Army.

FORGIVENESS

The church, while not preventing 'The Troubles' in Northern Ireland, did much to alleviate them and to eventually help bring peace. In addition, individual Christians such as Gordon Wilson displayed incredible acts of forgiveness. When the IRA bombed a memorial service in Enniskillen in 1987, killing 12 people including his daughter Marie, he showed public forgiveness towards her killers, despite having watched her die.

"She held my hand tightly, and gripped me as hard as she could. She said, 'Daddy, I love you very much.' Those were her exact words to me, and those were the last words I ever heard her say." To the astonishment of listeners, Wilson went on to add, *"But I bear no ill will. I bear no grudge. Dirty sort of talk is not going to bring her back to life. She was a great wee lassie. She loved her profession. She was a pet. She's dead. She's in heaven and we shall meet again. I will pray for these men tonight and every night."*

The impact of these words are widely considered the reason why there were no loyalist revenge attacks for the Enniskillen bombing.

FRIENDLY FIRE

Of the approximately 3,500 that have been killed as part of the Conflict in Northern Ireland over the last 40 years the vast majority (over 88%) were killed by paramilitary (also called terrorist) groups and most of the rest by the British Army or Royal Ulster Constabulary. Nearly 50,000 people were injured. Despite the fact that paramilitary groups were set up to protect their own religious communities, a significant number (often around a quarter) of those attacked and killed were from their own communities.

The Shared Future [of] Irish Churches

The history of the island of Ireland has been at times tragic but at other times inspirational, and for the last 1600 years the church has been an integral part of this history. The various denominations in Ireland today have varying beliefs and structures but they all share a common ancestry in that first gathering of church in the New Testament. And they all share a common bond in Jesus Christ.

Today, particularly with a more settled political climate, church denominations have renewed their commitment to work together in unity to tackle some of the many issues affecting people across Ireland. There is the continuing work in reconciliation, joint statements on social and political issues, collaboration in youth work, campaigning against poverty, debt and injustice and grass roots inter-church projects to better reach local communities.

While our shared past has, at times, been difficult there is an intention and hope in the churches today that our shared future will bring about a renewal of faith and hope for society across Ireland.

SHARED BUILDING

There are several examples across Ireland where 2 denominations (particularly the Protestant ones) actually share the same building, although they will tend to have separate services.

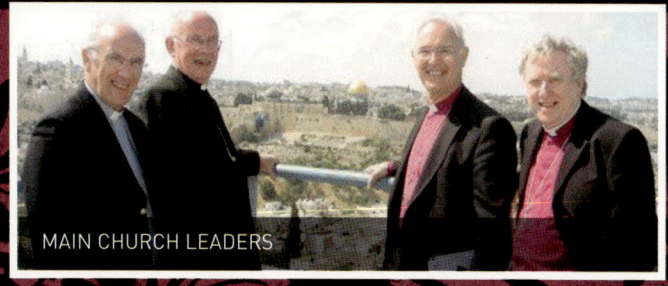

MAIN CHURCH LEADERS

REACHING THE CONTINENTS

Irish Christian youth organisations send 1000s of young people overseas each year to between 25-30 different countries in 5 continents! That's without even counting all those that join teams in Ireland!

THEY COULD LEARN A THING OR TWO

When the main denominations' leaders gather together each year they will often invite representatives from the other churches. This not only provides a welcome to each denomination in the other but also provides some accountability to others in how they are governed. It may also be to learn a thing or two from other denominations –but probably won't be admitted!

IRISH LANGUAGE

The Church of Ireland will also conduct some of its worship in Irish. It has a group **Cummann Galeach na hEaglaise (The Irish Guild of the Church)** that encourages the use of the Irish Language and has even published the Book of Common Prayer (its core book to guide worship) into Irish.

80%

In Northern Ireland over 80% of all voluntary youth work is church based.

5000

There are approximately **5,000 volunteers** working regularly with young people in the Church of Ireland. If they were paid an average hourly wage it would cost **£7,636,200 (€8.7m) per year!**

PART
2

The Church of Ireland Today

The Church of Ireland Today - Anglicanism

The Church of Ireland today is part of the worldwide communion of Anglican churches. This means that:

- They are in fellowship together and teach, worship and are organised in a similar way

- They have a common ancestry in the Church of England

- They have the Archbishop of Canterbury as their senior leader. However each country or province has its own Archbishop (in Ireland it is the Archbishop of Armagh)

There are 77 million Anglicans in the world, part of 38 National or provincial churches that operate as far away as New Zealand and Brazil.

The Church of Ireland has around 383,000 people who consider themselves members across over **450 Parishes** and **12 dioceses**. These parishes are smaller areas of land over which a Church of Ireland minister will be responsible. Each parish will have at least one church (governed by a Select Vestry) and smaller parishes are often grouped together.

A diocese is a larger area containing many parishes and administered by a bishop, who will also support and advise clergy as well as appointing new ones. Most dioceses will contain at least 1 Cathedral, which contains the Bishop's traditional 'seat' –symbolizing his role as a teacher.

The Church of Ireland is governed by the bishops and a group of representatives from the clergy and laity (people who aren't clergy), who meet every year to discuss church matters at a General Synod.

Despite the fact that Anglicanism started in England there are now more Anglicans in Africa than in England and the rest of the world combined.

The largest parish in Ireland is Shankill Parish, Lurgan in County Down. It serves 1400 families and the building holds 1,100 people.

The smallest church in Ireland is the Church of St. Gobban in County Antrim. It is privately owned as it can be hard to get a congregation into a church that is only 10 by 4 feet in size!

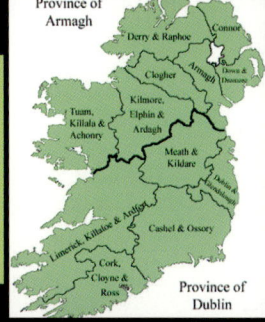

Every inch of Ireland is included in a parish. There is nowhere on the island that you could be and not be part of the responsibility of a local parish.

Christchurch Cathedral in Dublin has a display that still contains the mummified heart of its first Archbishop. Also on display are the mummified bodies of a cat and a rat that were found in the organ in 1860!

The Beliefs of the Church of Ireland

As the Church of Ireland has it roots in both the beginning of Celtic Christianity and also the Reformation it is regarded as both **Catholic and Protestant.**

The teaching of the Church of Ireland can be found in the **Book of Common Prayer and the 39 Articles** of Religion (written at the time of the Reformation in 1563).

The Church of Ireland way of looking at belief focuses on 3 areas:

1.Scripture –What does the Bible say about it?

2.Tradition –What has the Church understood about faith over many years?

3.Reason –How reason or understanding of belief is part of a living and real faith.

This means that the Church of Ireland endeavours to teach from the Bible, out of a rich heritage of Christian tradition

In addition the Church of Ireland also places much emphasis on the sacraments of Baptism and Holy Communion, which were given to the Church by Jesus Christ. It believes that it is through Baptism that God gives new life and through Holy Communion that God strengthens our life with Christ.

WHAT IS A SACRAMENT?

A sacrament is an outward and visible sign of an inward and invisible grace. In other words something we do on the outside that involves God working unseen but yet powerfully inside our lives.

DOESN'T THE CHURCH FALL OUT OVER ITS BELIEF?

Sometimes there are disagreements. The Church of Ireland has written beliefs –known as doctrine, and from time to time there will be differences as to how members interpret belief in light of scripture, tradition and reason. This is not a new development as even two of the great Apostles, Peter and Paul, disagreed as to how Jews and Gentiles (non-Jews) were to be treated. However it is important to note that they still continued working with each other to proclaim the Gospel.

WHAT IF I DON'T BELIEVE ALL THESE THINGS 100%?

All belief has an element of doubt and Jesus acknowledges (in Mark 9) the father of a young boy who says 'I do believe, help me overcome my unbelief!' Everyone doubts –it is important not to ignore doubts or questions but to communicate them to God and others. It is when we combine what belief we have in Christ with a desire to follow him that it becomes our Faith.

How We Worship As A Church

For a Christian, worship means **'to give worth'** to God –what we say and do in our lives to bring honour to God. A person can worship God as an individual but also in common fellowship with other Christians. This 'fellowship' or 'community' is the most basic definition of church –where Christians are described in Romans 12 (New Testament) as being all part of one body.

Most Christians will gather with each other on a regular basis to worship God –this could be anything from a Bible study to a youth group but it mainly involves a Sunday Worship Service in a church building.

Anglicans in the Church of Ireland tend to conduct their worship in church from a book called the **Book of Common Prayer (BCP)**. This contains many services for morning and evening prayer, Holy Communion, Baptism, marriage and so on including various prayers and readings. These services are **liturgical**, which means that there is a pattern to the worship, often with particular responses from the congregation.

Despite this liturgical framework however, there is much scope for worship to take place in the Church of Ireland in different ways (For instance through Family Services, Services of the Word and informal worship), meaning that a person's experience of worship can differ markedly from church to church

ISN'T WORSHIP JUST ABOUT SINGING?

Thankfully not! In Christianity worship is simply about us giving honour and worth to God –through every aspect of our lives such as praying, giving, praising and just trying to do the right thing. Worship in a Church of Ireland Service is the attempt to lead people to God in prayer and praise, to show that they are supported by his love and grace to help them lead a life that is honouring to God.

WHY ALL THE BOOKS?!

A Church of Ireland Service will often involve 3 (quite large!) books. –A Bible (for obvious reasons!), A hymnal containing the words and music for many of the hymns and worship songs sung and the Prayer Book to guide our worship. It is fairly common to see people pick up the wrong book during the service –and sometimes not realise for a minute or two!

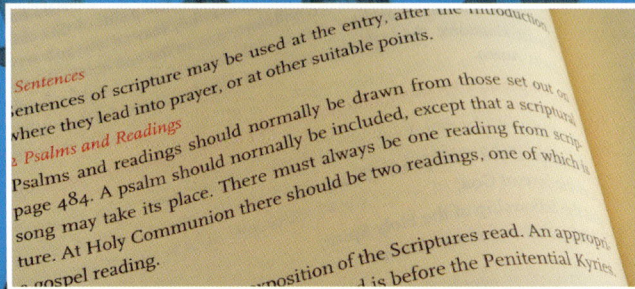

Sentences

Sentences of scripture may be used at the entry, after the introduction where they lead into prayer, or at other suitable points.

Psalms and Readings

Psalms and readings should normally be drawn from those set out on page 484. A psalm should normally be included, except that a scriptural song may take its place. There must always be one reading from scripture. At Holy Communion there should be two readings, one of which is a gospel reading.

...position of the Scriptures read. An appropri...d is before the Penitential Kyries.

A WORSHIP SERVICE:

- Expresses what Christians believe, from Biblical teaching.
- Helps people come closer to God and others as a 'Body' of Christ.
- Reminds the church of its mission to serve others.
- Can lead to those moments of wonder –where we feel connected to God in a way that words cannot explain.

More Than Just A Building

Church of Ireland buildings are more than just places of worship. They are designed to help us look to God and, if you look closely, many of them have **stories** to tell us.

Many church buildings will have been built over 100 years ago and some are still on the same site they have occupied for centuries. However, there are a significant number of more modern church buildings – often built as a result of church 'plants' in new areas or as a redevelopment of an older building.

The older churches will usually be built in stone with either a spire or tower. Often they will be in the shape of a cross, be East-facing and be surrounded (particularly in the countryside) by a cemetery. Modern churches have a much more varied design –some are rounded or square, and are often built alongside a hall or parish centre. They tend to be warmer than older church buildings!

There are certain features (see opposite) to look out for in a Church of Ireland that are common to all its buildings:

The Font: This is a special stand for holding water where baptisms are performed. It is usually near the door to symbolize a new member entering into the family of the church. A few churches even have larger water tanks for adult baptisms!

The Communion or Holy Table: This will be at the front of the church in what is called the Sanctuary and is where Communion is prepared and then given to worshipers.

The Lectern: This is a stand on which a Bible is placed and from where it is read to the congregation.

The Pulpit: This is an area from where the sermon is preached to the congregation and often had to be raised in order for the congregation to see and hear the minister.

Stained Glass Windows can be found in most, even modern, churches. They are often works of incredible artistry and can depict scenes and people from the Bible or the life of Saints. As it has only been in the last 100 years that reading and Bible ownership have become common, the windows acted as visual aids to help people understand their faith.

ON THE WINGS OF EAGLES

Many Lecterns have a Bible held up by an eagle -this is the symbol of John the Evangelist who proclaimed Christ as 'the Word of God' at the beginning of his Gospel. The flying eagle is thus a suitable emblem from which God's word is read, reaching the ends of the earth.

BUILDINGS OF COMMUNITY

Churches also serve a community function and many will have memorial plaques to remember those that have died in wars or previous Rectors. Some will have been placed there by the family of a person recently deceased. Some churches display the flags or emblems of organisations that are (or have been) involved in church life such as the Boy's Brigade or Mother's Union.

Many churches were built with the entrance facing west (where the sun sets) and the **Sanctuary** (with its stained glass window) facing east towards the rising sun. This meant that a person walking to the front would be going west to east, which symbolizes going from the evil of the present world to the glory of heaven to come.

The main part of the church where people sit is called the **Nave**. It is from the Latin word 'ship' because the ceiling of the church often looked like an upside-down hull (bottom of a ship).

Many older churches have a **bell tower** from which the bells are rung to 'call' people to worship or to celebrate a special event such as a wedding.

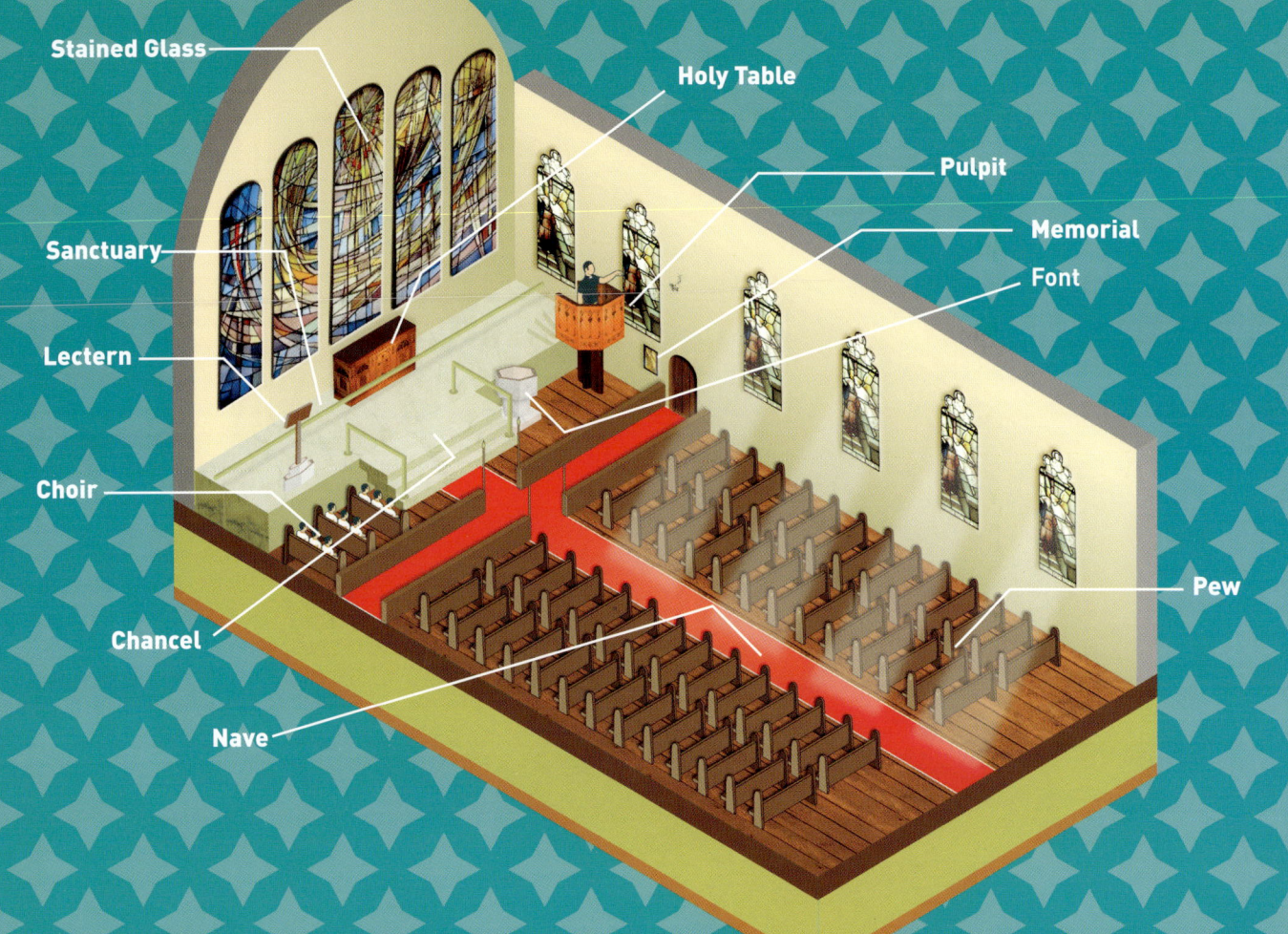

Stained Glass

Holy Table

Pulpit

Sanctuary

Memorial

Font

Lectern

Choir

Chancel

Pew

Nave

57

How We Worship

Sunday Morning and Evening Prayer will usually contain the following main elements:

Preparation: A time to listen to God, worship him and ask for forgiveness and grace

Ministry of the Word: The singing of a Psalm or Canticle (a worship song based on Bible verses), reading from the Bible and saying the Apostles' Creed (a statement of what we believe).

Prayers: The Lord's Prayer is said, a special prayer for the day is said (called a Collect) and the congregation joins in with these prayers. Prayers for the world about us and those in need are also said.

The Sermon: A time when the minister or other person is able to teach the church congregation.

Hymns: These are songs of worship and prayer and can be used from any source but usually from the Church of Ireland's Church Hymnal Book.

THE HOLY COMMUNION SERVICE

This is a Service that is similar to Morning Prayer in that it has the Ministry of the Word and prayers but it also contains the Act of Holy Communion based on Jesus' commands to His followers at the **Last Supper**. The bread and the wine of communion is received at the front of the church and the Service is regarded very highly in the Church of Ireland. Consequently many people do not receive Holy Communion until they understand some of its meaning and undertake some preparation to do so (usually, but not always, during a Confirmation Course). Holy Communion in the Church of Ireland is normally open to all those who are baptized and who have a professed faith in Christ, regardless of their background.

BAPTISM

Baptism is an ancient ceremony of admission into faith and Jesus himself was baptised in the river Jordan by John the Baptist. It is a sign of forgiveness (God washing away our sin), faith in Jesus Christ and acceptance into the family of believers.

In the church a person is baptised by having water poured over them (or being submersed in water) in the name of the Father, Son and Holy Spirit. Many people are baptised as infants, when their sponsors (parents and often God-parents) make promises to God on their behalf. They promise to raise the child as a Christian within the church until they are old enough to make a decision to follow Christ for themselves. This is often done at a Service of Confirmation.

CONFIRMATION

Confirmation is a special Service where a person confirms these promises made for them at Baptism. It is public decision to follow Jesus, usually made after attending a Confirmation preparation group. Often a young person or adult will have already made this decision in private but Confirmation is important not only because the decision is made with the support of the congregation but also because the Bishop lays his hand on each candidate and prays that the Holy Spirit will confirm them (make them stronger) in their faith.

As Confirmation preparation usually involves teaching about Holy Communion, most candidates will receive Holy Communion for the first time soon after they are confirmed.

INFANT BAPTISM

In the Church of Ireland baptism has mostly taken place when a person is a baby (infant Baptism) involving water being poured on the baby's head. However it is also common in the Christian church for a person to be baptised by being completely covered in water. This can mean using a small water tank in the floor of a church, a portable water tank (even a bath tub!) or moving the congregation to a local swimming pool, river or even the sea.

KNOW YOUR CATECHISM

Candidates for Confirmation in the Church of Ireland need to have a knowledge of its Catechism –which is basically a summary of its belief. Generally this means candidates knowing about the Apostles' Creed, 10 Commandments, Lord's Prayer and the Sacraments. In the older Catechism this would have involved learning the answers to 25 questions about belief. The first being 'What is your name?' and the rest being a lot harder!

THOUSANDS EVERY YEAR!

Somewhere between **2-3,000 young people are Confirmed in the Church of Ireland every single year** – many of them between the ages of 12 and 15. However there are also a lot of adults who are confirmed each year, either because they weren't confirmed as a young person, or came from a different church background. Many do simply because they have come to faith as adults and want to be baptised and then have their faith 'confirmed' by the Bishop.

The Catechism & Sacraments

The word 'catechism' literally means 'to sound down' or teach and is used to describe those basic beliefs that should be taught –particularly to young people. In the Church of Ireland the Catechism is an instruction that is supposed to be learned by every person before they are brought to be Confirmed by the Bishop. It takes the form of questions and answers and in it the Confirmation candidate (who will have been already baptised) will first affirm their baptism before professing a belief through the **Apostles' Creed, Ten Commandments, the Lord's Prayer and the Sacraments.**

What is a Sacrament? A sacrament is an outward and visible sign of an inward and spiritual grace. It is believed to be a religious action (the 'outward and visible') that conveys a blessing ('inward and spiritual grace') upon the believer who participates in it. The Church of Ireland, and the whole Anglican Church, believe there to be two Sacraments ordained (given special meaning) by Christ as being necessary for Salvation. In other words actions that need to be taken in order to restore our relationship with God and be forgiven.

The two Sacraments in the Church of Ireland are:

Baptism: This sacrament marks the start of a journey of faith, a repentance of sin and a turning away from evil and towards Christ. Often Baptism takes place when a person is just an infant and so the promises are made on their behalf by parents with the view that they will be 'Confirmed' when the person is older.

Holy Communion or The Lord's Supper: This sacrament commemorates the Last Supper, Christ's death and everything that we gain as a result of it. It is taken in remembrance of the bread and wine shared between Jesus and the disciples as a symbol of his body and blood.

The Apostles Creed

The Apostles' Creed is a statement of Christian belief shared by, and central to, Christian church denominations across the world. It gets its name because it was supposed to have been dictated by each of the 12 apostles, who each gave it an individual part. It is similar to the later Nicene Creed of 325AD, which clarified the belief in the Trinity. The Apostles' Creed is said at most Church of Ireland services while the Nicene Creed is said during a Holy Communion service.

A knowledge of and belief in the Apostles' Creed is central to the life of a Christian. The Christian faith is not simply a set of ideas or morals; rather it is established on the meaning and purpose of the life, death and resurrection of Jesus Christ. Therefore a belief in and knowledge of these historical facts surrounding Jesus Christ is essential. The Apostles' Creed also outlines the relationship between God the Father, God the Son (Jesus) and God the Holy Spirit and our belief in the importance of God's church, fellowship and our new life in Heaven.

Studying the Creed will help us to think more deeply about our own understanding of the Christian faith and hopefully equip us to explain it to others. It also serves to remind us that we are part of a community of Christians that reaches right back to the birth of the Church and the first Apostles who were appointed by Jesus himself. As one ancient writer wrote **"the Creed is the tie that binds us together."**

I BELIEVE IN GOD,

THE FATHER ALMIGHTY, CREATOR OF HEAVEN AND EARTH.

I BELIEVE IN JESUS CHRIST,

HIS ONLY SON, OUR LORD,

WHO WAS CONCEIVED BY THE HOLY SPIRIT,

BORN OF THE VIRGIN MARY,

SUFFERED UNDER PONTIUS PILATE,

WAS CRUCIFIED, DIED,

AND WAS BURIED;

HE DESCENDED INTO HELL.

ON THE THIRD DAY HE ROSE AGAIN;

HE ASCENDED INTO HEAVEN,

HE IS SEATED AT THE RIGHT HAND OF THE FATHER,

AND HE WILL COME AGAIN TO JUDGE THE LIVING AND THE DEAD.

I BELIEVE IN THE HOLY SPIRIT,

THE HOLY CATHOLIC CHURCH.

THE COMMUNION OF SAINTS,

THE FORGIVENESS OF SINS,

THE RESURRECTION OF THE BODY,

AND THE LIFE EVERLASTING.

AMEN.

65

The Lords Prayer

The Lord's Prayer is one of the commonly known elements of the Christian faith. A prayer that was given to us by Jesus as part of a great sermon he preached to his disciples from a mountainside (the Sermon on the Mount) and that is still taught today. It sums up how we should pray and relate to God every day and is a key part of Church Services.

OUR FATHER IN HEAVEN, HALLOWED BE YOUR NAME

The prayer asks us to approach God as 'Daddy' (The word 'Abba' in the original Aramaic) but also to remember that he is in Heaven, is all-powerful and that he should be regarded as Holy.

YOUR KINGDOM COME, YOUR WILL BE DONE, ON EARTH AS IT IS IN HEAVEN.

We use this prayer to ask that God's purpose –His Kingdom, be apparent in everything. That the great things that occur in a perfect heaven would be done on earth –and that we might undertake them!

GIVE US THIS DAY OUR DAILY BREAD.

It is also a prayer that God would provide for our daily needs –not just our physical needs like food and shelter but for our spiritual needs like hope and a purpose.

FORGIVE US OUR SINS AS WE FORGIVE THOSE WHO SIN AGAINST US.

This is perhaps the hardest part for many of us to pray –that we ask God to take away and forget about our sin just as we do the same for other people that hurt us. God forgives us that we might go to heaven –do we then forgive others?

LEAD US NOT INTO TEMPTATION BUT DELIVER US FROM EVIL.

Our 'temptation' is when we are tested in our faith to do unworthy or sinful things. God will sometimes allow this in order to strengthen our faith but always give us what we need to pass the test (1 Corinthians 10:13).

This prayer is asking that God doesn't let us endure tests or trials before we are ready for them. However, it also asks that God sets us free from evil -all those fears and sins and selfish habits that we have, but also from the work of the Devil -a fallen angel who is the enemy of God and humanity.

FOR THE KINGDOM THE POWER AND THE GLORY ARE YOURS NOW AND FOREVER. AMEN.

These words are not contained in the original prayer taught to us by Jesus. They have been added by Christians (not all though –for instance the Roman Catholic church does not use them) as a conclusion to the prayer and mean that we regard God as sovereign.

In other words, that everything belongs to him, that he has power over everything and decides everything (including the decision to let us direct our own lives –for better or worse). And that this will always be the case. The finish to the prayer -'Amen' has come to mean 'It is true' or 'so be it' and is used to affirm God.

'If somebody said, give me a summary of Christian faith on the back of an envelope, the best thing to do would be to write Our Lord's Prayer'.
Rowan Williams, Archbishop of Canterbury.

The Ten Commandments

From the time that the very first sin separated mankind from God, He designed a plan to restore our relationship and fellowship with him. This plan, given to Israel, was called a **covenant** and was to be shared with the whole world. The covenant meant that God's people would agree to obey a spoken and written set of obligations and responsibilities (laws) to demonstrate their devotion to God and separation from sin. At the very core of these laws were the 10 Commandments -a moral code given to Moses on two stone tablets on **Mount Sinai** after the people of Israel had been freed from Egypt.

The Commandments and other laws were designed to lead Israel to a life of practical holiness. In them,
people could see the nature of God and His plan for how they should live. By Jesus' time however, many people looked at the laws the wrong way –they thought that to obey every law was to earn prosperity and protection from invasion or disaster. Law keeping became an end in itself and not the means to draw closer to God. Jesus pointed out that while the **law was important in revealing who God is and how to follow him**, it would ultimately be through Jesus that people would be restored to God. He had come to fulfil the Law and not abolish it. Therefore Christians regard both the Old and New Testaments highly.

The 10 Commandments (shortened version) from Exodus Chapter 20

1. YOU SHALL HAVE **NO OTHER GODS** BEFORE ME
2. YOU SHALL NOT **MAKE FOR YOURSELF AN IDOL**
3. YOU SHALL NOT **MISUSE THE NAME OF THE LORD** YOUR GOD
4. REMEMBER THE **SABBATH** BY KEEPING IT HOLY
5. HONOUR YOUR **FATHER AND MOTHER**
6. YOU SHALL NOT **MURDER**
7. YOU SHALL NOT COMMIT **ADULTERY**
8. YOU SHALL NOT **STEAL**
9. YOU SHALL NOT GIVE **FALSE TESTIMONY**
10. YOU SHALL NOT **COVET**

The Church Year

Worship in the Church of Ireland follows a calendar throughout the year with each Sunday having a theme, a Collect prayer and a set of readings. The year is divided up into seasons so that all the main events in the life of Jesus can be celebrated. Don't forget that for much of the history of the Church of Ireland people didn't have access to Bibles or simply couldn't read. The layout of the Church year was designed to bring our faith to life and help us remember day to day the birth, ministry, death and resurrection of Jesus Christ.

The Church year starts on Advent Sunday (Four Sundays before Christmas) and follows:

ADVENT: A time of preparation for the coming of Jesus. This season lasts for 4 Sundays and often involves many traditions like the lighting of an Advent candle on each of these Sundays to symbolize God's progressive revelation of himself leading to Jesus as the light of the world.

CHRISTMAS: The celebration of the birth of Jesus. This season starts at sunset on Christmas Eve and lasts through to January 5th –the 12 days of Christmas. January 5th became known as the 12th night and traditionally is the night we are supposed to take our Christmas decorations down!

EPIPHANY: A time to remember that Jesus came to save the whole world. This is celebrated on January 6th and remembers the coming of the wise men bringing gifts to the Christ child and revealing him to the world as Christ and King.

The Church Year - Lent

A period to remember the 40 days Jesus spent fasting in the desert in preparation for His ministry. It begins on Ash Wednesday and ends on the Saturday before Easter Sunday. It is actually 46 days long but the Sundays are not counted. Christians traditionally use it as a time for self-examination, prayer, repentance and fasting as they prepare to celebrate the resurrection of Christ.

Many churches will fast on particular days during lent and also many Christians will fast certain things such as meat, alcohol, sweets or even a favourite activity (such as watching TV) during it. The point of this being to replace what you are giving up with prayer. Sundays in Lent are regarded as Feast days so there is no Fasting.

Lent starts on Ash Wednesday, which gets its name from the practice of placing ashes on the foreheads of Christians as a sign of repentance. This comes from the Biblical example of dusting oneself with ashes as a sign of sorrow for sins and faults. It is a practice that only tends to happen in the Roman Catholic Church today and the Church of Ireland uses Ash Wednesday as a day of Fasting.

The day before Ash Wednesday is called **Shrove Tuesday, Pancake Tuesday or Mardi Gras (Fat Tuesday).** Traditionally people fasted in Lent from many rich foods such as eggs, milk and fat so this day was used as a Feast Day to use up what was still left in the cupboard –**particularly to make Pancakes!**

In the Church of Ireland Holy Week in this season is also regarded very importantly as commemorating the last week of the earthly life of Jesus. It begins on **Palm Sunday**, the Sunday before Easter Sunday, which remembers Jesus being welcomed into Jerusalem by the people as a King by laying Palm fronds across his path. Also that he rode into the city on a donkey to emphasize the importance of humility. Many Church of Ireland churches will often hold a service on each day of Holy week.

On **Maundy Thursday** we remember the Last Supper that Jesus shared with His disciples, when he asked them to remember him (through the taking the bread and wine in Holy Communion) and when he gave them a mandate to love one another ('Maundy' comes from the word 'mandate').

The most important day of Holy Week is **Good Friday** when the church remembers the arrest, torture, crucifixion, death and burial of Jesus. It is a solemn time for Christians as they remember the sacrifice that Jesus made so that their own sins could be forgiven and their relationship with God restored. However it is also with the hope of what happened 3 days after the crucifixion.

The Church Year
-Easter

The day and season of Easter is a celebration of the resurrection of Jesus Christ from the dead and the defeat of death, meaning that those who choose to follow Christ would 'not perish (die) but have eternal life' (John 3:16). In other words that our earthly bodies may die but our soul (who we really are) will get a new body in Heaven where we will live forever. This is central to the belief and life of Christians and so Easter Sunday is regarded as the most important day of the year.

The date of Easter is actually calculated according to a lunar calendar (in a system dating from 325AD) and so can happen any time from March 22nd to April 25th each year. This also means that all the other dates related to Easter, such as Ash Wednesday and Ascension, will also change. It means too that the school Easter holidays are on different dates each year!

Also in the Easter season is Ascension Day, which happens 40 days after Easter Sunday on a Thursday. It remembers the 40 days that Jesus spent with His followers after he was resurrected, his 'Great Commission' to take the Gospel message to the world and then his ascension up to heaven.

The end of the Easter season is marked by Pentecost. Jesus told his followers that after he ascended to heaven they would get a 'helper' –the Holy Spirit who would live in Christians to call, challenge, inspire, comfort and enable them.

10 days after the ascension (50 after Easter – Pentecost means 'fifty') the Holy Spirit came upon Christ's followers in Jerusalem in such a powerful way that 3,000 extra people believed in God and were baptised. Pentecost therefore is also known as the birthday of the Church.

The Church Year — Ordinary Time

The rest of the year (mostly between Pentecost and Advent) for the Anglican Church is known as **Ordinary time**. The 'Ordinary' doesn't mean 'common' but rather 'counted time' (from the word 'ordinal) as the Sundays in this season are counted up until Advent.

These Sundays in Ordinary Time are often used to focus on various aspects of Christian faith but especially the mission of the Church in the world.

Ordinary time includes **Trinity Sunday** –which celebrates the belief in God as 3 persons and also All Saints Day –which remembers the work of all those

Christians (saints) in the past that have faithfully followed Christ. **All Saints Day** is the day after Halloween on 1st November and although Halloween is more well known it is actually named from 'hallow' ('Holy' or 'saint') and 'een' ('eve' or evening before).

Also of note during this period of the year will be a **Harvest Thanksgiving Service** held to thank God for his provision of food to us and to remind us of our dependence on him. It is a service of rejoicing and often the church will be decorated with food harvested that autumn which is then given to the needy.

Each season also has a colour. These colours are often displayed in the church – on the Communion Table, Lectern or even as the colour of the minister's vesture (outer clothing). The colours are used as a symbol of the season and to remind people what church season of the year they are in.

ADVENT: Purple which is the colour of royalty to welcome the advent (coming) of the King

CHRISTMAS: White is used to symbolize purity, holiness and virtue.

EPIPHANY: White is also used and symbolizes celebration and newness

LENT: Purple is used to symbolize the pain and suffering leading up to the crucifixion of Jesus. Easter: White is used to celebrate the newness of the resurrection.

PENTECOST: Red is used on this day to symbolize the presence of God.

ORDINARY TIME: Green to symbolize new life and growth in the church and in the resurrection.

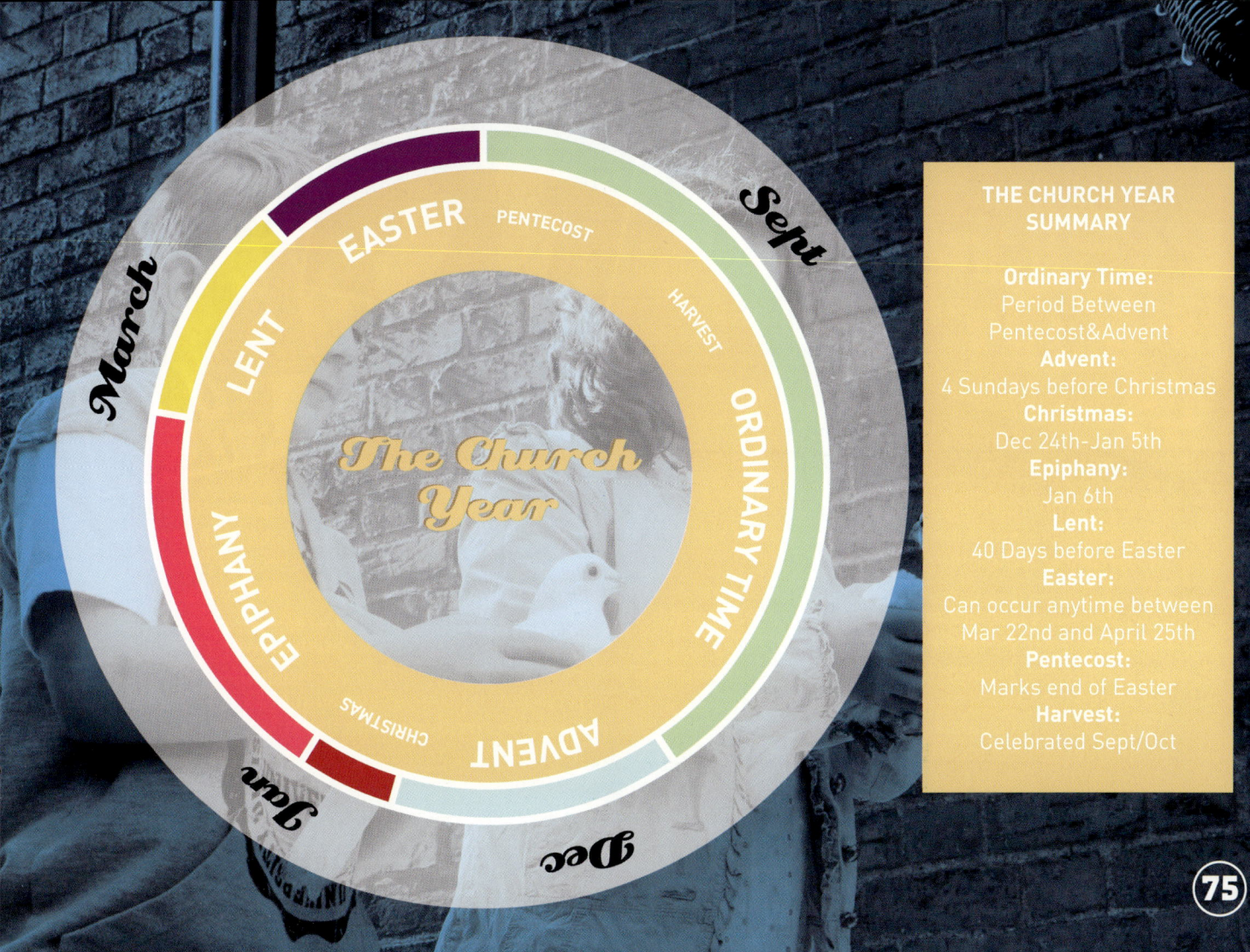

EASTER
PENTECOST
HARVEST
ORDINARY TIME
ADVENT
CHRISTMAS
EPIPHANY
LENT

The Church Year

Sept
Dec
Jan
March

THE CHURCH YEAR SUMMARY

Ordinary Time:
Period Between Pentecost&Advent
Advent:
4 Sundays before Christmas
Christmas:
Dec 24th-Jan 5th
Epiphany:
Jan 6th
Lent:
40 Days before Easter
Easter:
Can occur anytime between Mar 22nd and April 25th
Pentecost:
Marks end of Easter
Harvest:
Celebrated Sept/Oct

75

People in the Church of Ireland

Every member of the Church has a service to give to God and a place to take up in the life, worship and governance of the Church.

The people of God are often referred to as lay people or Laity (from the Greek word 'Laos', meaning people). From among the Laity some are called or ordained (set apart) for special tasks of ministry. These ordained ministers are called clergy and the Church of Ireland has three different orders of clergy: Deacon, Priest and Bishop –all of which are open to both men and women.

A Deacon is ordained by a Bishop for a particular ministry and usually as a first step in the process of becoming a priest. Deacons can lead church services but cannot celebrate Holy Communion.

A Priest is ordained by a Bishop (with several other Priests present) with his or her primary task being to proclaim the Gospel and administer the Sacraments. This is normally done as the Pastor of a parish where they will have responsibility for its spiritual life.

A Bishop is the chief Pastor for a number of parishes, which together are called his diocese. A bishop is consecrated by at least 3 other bishops.

WHAT ARE ALL THESE OTHER TITLES?!

Rectors and Vicars: This is usually the main minister in a parish.

Curates: This is an assistant to the Rector/Vicar. Parishes used to be described as a 'Cure (Old English for 'Care') of Souls' and from this we get 'Curate'.

Canons: This is a position related to the Cathedral in a Diocese. A minister with this title will help to administer a Cathedral and have a special seat there!

Deans: This is the minister in charge of a Cathedral.

Archdeacons: There tends to be only one Archdeacon in each diocese and as well as also having a seat (called a stall) in the Cathedral they will also tend to work closely with the Bishop.

Canons, Deans and Archdeacons will also usually have the responsibility of a parish where they are Rector.

WHAT IS THE ROLE OF THE CLERGY?

The main duties of the clergy can vary from place to place but they generally involve:

- Teaching and preaching
- Administering baptism and communion
- Leading church services
- Preparing sermons
- Visiting the sick and bereaved
- Other services such as marriages and funerals
- Managing staff and volunteers
- Implementing vision and direction for the parish
- Dealing with problems and issues
- Pastoral visits to church members
- Inter-church and community meetings
- Assisting church programmes such as Youth Groups
- School visits and management
- Encouraging new leaders and volunteers
- Preparation classes for marriage, baptism and confirmation

The Mission of the Church of Ireland

The Church of Ireland doesn't just exist to meet on a Sunday morning –it is part of God's mission to the world. It seeks to proclaim the Good News (Gospel) of the Kingdom, reach, baptise and nurture new believers and to meet needs, serve others and transform injustice in society –to demonstrate the heart of God to the world around it. This is no small task! Each diocese, church and individual Christian should also be seeking to undertake God's mission or plan for them.

Traditionally the mission of the Church of Ireland has been concentrated in the work of ministers as they pastor (tend the needs of) their parishioners 'from the cradle to the grave' and also through its rich tradition of sending missionaries to spread Christianity to other parts of the world. It has also sought to fulfil the Great Commission through the everyday witness of its members.

Today the Church of Ireland carries on this tradition and is involved in most areas of community life; with people of all ages and backgrounds and in tackling a great variety of issues from education to the environment and from reconciliation to poverty. This involves clergy, youth workers, community workers, worship leaders, children's workers, administrators and many others, but consistently relies on the dedication of ordinary church members who seek to serve God by serving others.

79

How is the Church of Ireland Governed?

PARISH LEVEL:

Each parish will have a register of **General Vestry members** who must be over 18 years and be part of the parish. This General Vestry must meet once per year at Easter time at a meeting called the Easter Vestry. There they will elect a Select Vestry of up to 12 members with an additionally elected **Glebe Warden** and **Churchwarden**. The Rector will also appoint a Glebe Warden and Churchwarden.

The **Select Vestry** is responsible for providing all that is needed for the worship and work of the parish. This usually means control of the finance, buildings and furniture (or furnishings, fabric and finance –the 3 'Fs'). The Churchwardens are responsible for keeping control of the church service and collecting the offering. Glebe Wardens are responsible for the care and management of any church property and land.

Every third year the parish also elects people to the Diocesan Synod and also Parochial nominators who will help appoint a new Rector if there is a vacancy.

DIOCESAN LEVEL:

The Diocese meets at a **Diocesan Synod** which consists of the Bishop, clergy and between 2 and 5 lay (non-clergy) representatives from each parish for each clergyperson. The Synod meets once a year and looks after the 3 'Fs' for the diocese. It can also form various committees to work on its behalf and elects a council to manage its day-to-day work

Diocesan Synod will elect representatives to the General Synod.

WHOLE CHURCH:

The whole church is represented by the **General Synod**. It has 2 'Houses', a House of Bishops (12 in all from each diocese) and a House of Representatives drawn from every diocese with 2 laity for each clergy. The General Synod can make laws that affect the whole church. It is the only body that can alter the worship or doctrine (beliefs) of the Church of Ireland or express its opinion.

From the General Synod a Standing Committee is elected to administer its affairs on a day-to-day basis and a Representative Church Body is formed to control the finances of the central church and to hold property for the Church of Ireland.

General Vestry

Select Vestry

🟠 RECTOR

🔴🔴 X2 CHURCH WARDENS

🟡🟡 X2 GLEBE WARDENS

 X12 OTHER MEMBERS

Diocesan Synod

🟣 BISHOP

🟠🟠🟠🟠 CLERGY

2 LAY REPRESENTATIVES FOR EACH CLERGY MEMBER

Parochial Nominators

 X4 LAY PERSONS

General Synod

HOUSE OF BISHOPS

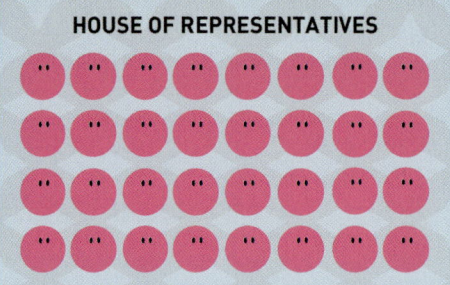

HOUSE OF REPRESENTATIVES

CLERGY

The Future of the Church of Ireland

The Church of Ireland over its history has had to face many challenges –external threats such as invasion and political upheaval and also challenges from within on how it could better treat those around it. For despite the good works of the church there are also times when it has not functioned as it should have.

And today and in our future there will continue to be challenges ahead –on how we engage with people and issues, how we serve others and point them to the very reason for our existence, Jesus Christ.

Whatever the future, it will be built upon the faith of those ordinary people, young and old, who do extra-ordinary things as they play their part in the body of Christ.

ACKNOWLEDGEMENTS:

I am grateful for the idea for this book, which came from clergy in Down and Dromore Diocese who asked questions about how we ensure future generations have an understanding of where their church came from –and what part they can play in it today. I hope this helps!

A lot advice and encouragement has been given to me over the course of this project and (with apologies to those mistakenly left out) I would like to thank the following people:

Andi McCarroll for not burying his talent in the ground and for always coming up with the right design –with a notable exception!

The members of DDYC who listened to me go on about this project for around 2 years –namely Katy, Ciara, Adrian, Martin, Peter, Jayne, Natalie, Rachel, Andy, Dave, Simon and Robert.

My colleagues in Down and Dromore who have encouraged this project and also asked the right questions –namely Bishop Harold, Philip, Mary, Margaret and Annette. You're welcome to use my deluxe office anytime!

My colleagues in parish and diocesan youth ministry who have given me valuable feedback on this project and particularly those who read the first draft and sent back their thoughts –Jonny Phenix, Steven Brickenden and Scott Evans.

Various others who took the time to read the draft and give me their thoughts –David Brown, Rev. Ian W. Ellis, Kenneth Milne and Francis Boyd.

Church of Ireland Publishing –particularly Susan Hood and the Literature Committee

All the young people in St. John's Youth Fellowship who looked over the initial designs and text – particularly Peter McKeown, Joleen Carlisle and Laureen Montgomery who actually took it as homework! Our young people have the unique ability to inspire and infuriate at the same time (!) -it is a privilege to know them.

My wife Lynne -for reasons too numerous to mention. She is the greater part of me.
And Emily, Elizabeth and Grace who make me feel every day like I've been given a million pounds to spend.

Our Lord and Saviour Jesus Christ.

Image Attributions:
Page 22 "Constantine" Alaskan Dude
Page 26 "Statue of Saint Patrick" Dyler Pillar
Page 71 "Christ" Georgy N Joseph

Sources: The author wishes to acknowledge various sources consulted in writing this book but particularly:

'A look at the Church of Ireland'
by Rev Robert Neill and Ven Philip Patterson

'A Short History of the Church of Ireland'
by Kenneth Milne

'The Christians -An Illustrated History'
by Tim Dowley

Written by:

Andrew Brannigan
Church of Ireland House
61-67 Donegall Street
Belfast BT1 2QH

Tel: +44 28 90240316
Mob: 07950 846621
E-mail: Andrew@downanddromore.org
Website: www.ddyc.co.uk